Going for the Gold

Other Books by Jeffrey L. Buller

A Toolkit for College Professors (with Robert E. Cipriano)
A Toolkit for Department Chairs (with Robert E. Cipriano)

Going for the Gold

How to Become a World-Class Academic Fundraiser

Jeffrey L. Buller and Dianne M. Reeves

ROWMAN & LITTLEFIELD
Lanham • Boulder • New York • London

Published by Rowman & Littlefield

A wholly owned subsidiary of The Rowman & Littlefield Publishing Group, Inc.
4501 Forbes Boulevard, Suite 200, Lanham, Maryland 20706
www.rowman.com

Unit A, Whitacre Mews, 26-34 Stannary Street, London SE11 4AB

British Library Cataloguing in Publication Information Available

Library of Congress Cataloging-in-Publication Data is Available

ISBN 978-1-4758-3155-9 (cloth: alk. paper)
ISBN 978-1-4758-3156-6 (pbk: alk. paper)
ISBN 978-1-4758-3157-3 (electronic)

♾™ The paper used in this publication meets the minimum requirements of American
National Standard for Information Sciences—Permanence of Paper for Printed Library
Materials, ANSI/NISO Z39.48-1992.

Printed in the United States of America

Dedication

To all the benefactors who put their trust in us, gave us the confidence to dream ever more ambitious dreams, and helped us build our university's largest endowment despite being our university's smallest college.

Table of Contents

Introduction   1

1   An Introduction to Academic Fundraising   5

2   Ethical Issues in Fundraising   23

3   Why One Size Does Not Fit All   43

4   The SPORT of Giving and the ACID Test   67

5   Raising Awareness, Not Just Money   85

6   Listening to and Telling Stories   109

Appendix A: Finding, Hiring, and Evaluating a Development Officer   131

Appendix B: AFP Code of Ethical Principles and Standards of
             Professional Practice   137

Appendix C: Donor Bill of Rights   141

Appendix D: Training at Your Institution   143

About the Authors   145

Introduction

Thank you for "getting it!" Thank you for understanding that, in order to be successful as a fundraiser in higher education today, you have to move outside your comfort zone. Faculty members and administrators realize that no one is just going to hand them money for that research project they care so much about. They have to present their goals to people who may not have been on a college campus since they graduated—or who may never have been on a college campus at all—and who may look at the world very differently from how a professor might. They have to realize that all the talk they hear in development meetings about booking gifts and restricted annuities isn't just "bean counting." Those "beans" are what will make their visions a reality.

Conversely, development officers (DOs) have to understand that the way decisions are made in the academic world are likely to be different from how they make decisions in their own offices. Having a curricular proposal approved can take an agonizingly long time. Department chairs and deans may technically be someone's "boss," but that word doesn't mean the same thing that it does in your world. You may feel perfectly at home in a corporate boardroom; perhaps you even have a corporate background yourself. That same setting, however, might feel very foreign to someone whose world consists largely of libraries, art studios, or chemistry labs. And how English professors see the world may be different from how faculty members in accounting, nursing, education, or engineering see the world. Your assumptions about people's motivations may be just as baffling to them as theirs may be to you.

And yet members of both the academic world and the development world have to work together. Fundraising in higher education is something that no one engages in alone. The different offices of a college or university have to understand one another and pool their talents if they hope to succeed

1

at developing programs for the future. In short, fundraising is not a "me" activity; it is a "we" activity, and we all have to see the world through one another's eyes.

Trends in how best to engage community members, potential donors, and alumni change constantly. From telephone banks to events to social media, everyone seems to be talking about *market segmentation*. But all that segmentation can leave the different parts of the institution moving in separate directions. If they want to go for the gold, they have to learn how to move in the same direction. That's why we created this book. As academic administrators and DOs, we learned early in our working relationship how each other's perspective was necessary in order for us to identify the best approach to take. And so, we decided to share those insights with others involved in academic fundraising.

These are exciting times in higher education and, with increasing competition for financial support, academic fundraisers face a lot of obstacles. But not having the right tools shouldn't be one of them. We wrote *Going for the Gold* to provide you with a toolkit of practical, field-tested approaches that can be used immediately. Our strategies are rooted in well-established studies but, more importantly, proven to work by our own experience. These are techniques that we've found useful, and we hope you will too.

Courses, workshops, and seminars in academic fundraising might want to adopt *Going for the Gold* as a guide or textbook. Presidents and provosts might consider giving a copy of it to every new dean, director, and department chair on their staff. And vice presidents for advancement or community engagement might encourage the entire development staff to read it as a way of understanding the perspective of academic leaders, a point of view that is sometimes significantly different from their own and often overlooked.

Like its companion volume *World-Class Fundraising Isn't a Spectator Sport, Going for the Gold* shares a number of stories that are adapted from the "real world" and that highlight experiences we've had working with academic administrators, DOs, and prospects or donors. Those incidents that we describe as witnessing ourselves always have a solid core of truth, but we've found it necessary to change certain details to protect the identities of those involved. In other cases, incidents have been conflated for the sake of concision.

For this reason, although the external details of a story may have been changed somewhat, all the basic plotlines relate to incidents we were involved in ourselves or saw unfold at our institutions. (We're embarrassed to admit that some of the people who made the mistakes in these case studies actually were we ourselves.) Regardless of whether the case study is intended to provide a positive or a negative example, our goal is always to illustrate ways in which you can improve the level of collaboration between the academic and development sectors of your school and demonstrate greater effectiveness, productivity, efficiency, and adherence to the highest ethical standards.

Each chapter concludes with a list of references (works cited in the chapter) and resources (works that haven't explicitly been cited but that can provide further information about the topics covered in that chapter). Four appendices at the end of the book offer additional material that anyone working in academic fundraising will find useful.

Both authors have numerous people to thank for their contributions to this book. Noteworthy among this group of generous colleagues are Bhagyashree Kundalkar for providing technical assistance, Sandy Ogden for her editorial insights, Ayn Patrick for helping with data input, and Magna Publications for allowing the authors to adapt and reuse in Chapters 3 and 5 some material that originally appeared in *Academic Leader*. (Reprint permission was granted by Magna Publications and *Academic Leader*.)

Jeffrey L. Buller and Dianne M. Reeves
Jupiter, Florida
May 15, 2016

Chapter One

An Introduction to Academic Fundraising

If you work in higher education today, it doesn't matter what title appears in your job description: You're a fundraiser. Large or small, public or private, old and historical or new and experimental, the institution you work for relies on external funding for a significant part of its budget. If you serve in the public sector, you already know the degree to which state funding for university systems has been diminished. From 2008 through 2014, state funding for higher education decreased 18.9%. In Wyoming, reductions in a single year (2013–2014) reached 7.4%. From 2009 through 2014, Louisiana endured the largest reduction in state appropriations per full-time equivalent student (39.4%), whereas Illinois witnessed the largest increase (49.5%). That increase, however, was intended to compensate for a long history of underfunding the state's pension program and is, thus, a bit misleading. (www.sheeo.org/sites/default/files/project-files/SHEF%20FY%20 2014-20150410.pdf.)

In 2015 and 2016, the inability of the governor and legislature in Illinois to reach a budget agreement created an extended period when the state government provided no support to higher education. Universities were, thus, compelled to lay off staff, decrease scholarship support, explore taking on more debt, or close their doors entirely. (www.chicagotribune.com/news/local/politics/ct-bruce-rauner-illinois-budget-universities-met-20151101-story.html and prospect.org/article/ illinois-universities-face-closures-layoffs-state-budget-impasse-continues.)

Forty-eight states—all except Alaska and North Dakota—are spending less per student than they did before the [2008] recession. . . . Public colleges and universities across the country have increased tuition to compensate for declining state funding and rising costs. Annual published tuition at four-year

5

public colleges has risen by $1,936, or 28 percent, since the 2007-08 school year, after adjusting for inflation. In Arizona, published tuition at four-year schools is up more than 80 percent, while in two other states—Florida and Georgia—published tuition is up more than 66 percent. (cbpp.org/research/states-are-still-funding-higher-education-below-pre-recession-levels.)

The result is that most funding for public universities now comes from four major areas: state revenue (usually in the range of 15–30%), tuition (30–45%), philanthropy (25–40%), and sponsored research (2–5%). (See Textbox 1.1.)

A familiar joke among college administrators goes like this. A prospective donor asks a dean, "Why are you coming to me for money? I thought your school was state-funded." The dean replies, "Well, we used to be state-funded. Then there was a round of budget cuts, and we became 'state-assisted.' A few years later, we had another round of budget cuts, and we became 'state-located.' After the last round of budget cuts, I guess we're now what you'd call 'state-tolerated.'"

Because flagship and other "name brand" universities make front page news inside and outside the academic world by succeeding in campaigns that raise more than a billion dollars at a time, many people—even many legislators and trustees—have come to believe that their own regional university is probably doing just fine and doesn't require as much support as it received in the past. In fact, the fundraising success of some top-tier universities may have impaired the ability of smaller schools to obtain state or federal funding. Even if they're working at a college or university that's largely tuition driven, administrators are sometimes asked, "Why don't you just spend more out of your endowment?"

The result is that public colleges, universities, and community colleges today are placed in a double bind: They have trouble raising external funds because the public feels that they're "state supported," and they have trouble increasing state support because governors and legislators think that they're funded by large endowments.

In the private sector, similar challenges exist. People hear about the size of the endowments at Harvard, Yale, Princeton, Stanford, and MIT and assume that all private colleges have access to similar resources. Even worse, stories about rates for tuition, housing, and fees that exceed $60,000 at educational institutions such as Middlebury College, Sarah Lawrence, George Washington University, and Vassar College lead many members of the public to believe that even small liberal arts colleges in their community are adequately supported since every student pays the full amount of the tuition posted on the website.

But the fact of the matter is that many private colleges have endowments that are quite small and that most private schools discount their tuition to such an extent that few, if any, students actually end up paying the full price advertised in recruitment materials. As a result, many schools find themselves conducting perpetual campaigns where annual fund appeals are combined with solicitations for major gifts to the endowment or general budget.

Private institutions have historically focused on cultivating new donors by soliciting alumni and building strong ties with a select group of major benefactors. Even though a great deal of this work is performed directly by staff members in the offices of development and alumni affairs, academic administrators still play a vital role in providing information about current and planned programs, setting priorities, and explaining to potential donors how their philanthropic interests relate to the school's larger mission. (See Textbox 1.2.)

The public and private sectors in higher education have historically misunderstood one another's funding, with each regarding the other as better off. Many private colleges envy their public counterparts because "they get all that state money." And many public institutions envy those in the private sector because "they get all that high tuition revenue." In fact, state support of public universities is lower than many people believe and is often reduced by the legislature as a cost-cutting measure. Similarly, few students pay the advertised price for tuition at most private colleges, and discounted tuition is sometimes not significantly higher than what out-of-state students pay at a public university. The result is that everyone in higher education depends on external support. Few college administrators can succeed without gaining at least some fundraising experience and few academic fundraisers can succeed if they don't understand the unique organizational culture of the college or university.

The result is that public and private universities must increasingly use the same strategies to pay their expenses. They raise their rates of tuition (risking strong public condemnation and discounting tuition for some who can't afford the full cost of attending college), increase fees, seek new populations of students, apply for grants, and involve larger and larger segments of the institutional community in fundraising.

Expecting more people to raise funds has a lot of benefits, but it brings problems too. Those who work on the academic side of the institution speak their own language and bring their own perspectives to the work of development that full-time fundraisers may not share. Conversely, the development side of the institution has its own way of viewing the world and its own vocabulary that may seem foreign to many faculty members and academic leaders. For that reason, let's take a brief look at how the world of fundraising works in case you're new to this activity. If you're currently a development officer (DO) and want to know more about the academic side of the house, you may want to skip ahead to the next section.

A PRIMER ON FUNDRAISING FOR FACULTY MEMBERS AND ACADEMIC ADMINISTRATORS

Development activities are such an integral part of higher education today—particularly in the United States—that it seems natural to ask: How did formal fundraising originate? The interesting answer is that, although its roots are quite ancient, the form in which we know it today is surprisingly new. Formal fundraising has a long history because almost every society known throughout history has had at least some tradition of making voluntary contributions to support a public good.

In ancient Athens, private funding paid for the tragic festivals at which the works of authors such as Aeschylus, Sophocles, and Euripides were performed. Each year, one of the public officials would select three wealthy individuals and assign one to each of the three playwrights as a way of paying for that author's performances. The person who was chosen was given the title *choregos* or "chorus leader," not because he physically led the chorus, but because his funding brought the performance to the public. The *choregos* usually regarded this opportunity as a great honor because of the prestige it conveyed within the community. It was the ancient equivalent of being named a supporting patron of an opera company or music festival.

Almsgiving also plays a central role in many religious traditions, including the Hindu (*bhiksha*), Buddhist (*dāna*), Hebrew (*zedakah*), Christian (*eleēmosunē*), and Muslim (*zakat*) faiths. Educational endowments traditionally trace their origins to 176 CE, when the Roman emperor Marcus Aurelius established four endowed chairs in the philosophical schools of Athens, one each for the Academy (founded by Plato), the Lyceum (founded by Aristotle), the Garden (founded by Epicurus), and the Stoic School (founded by Zeno of Citium).

In the United States, external funding for universities dates back to 1643, when Lady Ann Radcliffe Mowlson provided Harvard College with a gift of 100 English pounds to help support needy scholars. But for many years, this type of gift was usually fairly small and not a specifically designated part of the budget at most schools. The type of substantial, sustained support that colleges and universities receive from foundations and donors today became common only in the twentieth century.

In 1911, Andrew Carnegie established the Carnegie Foundation of New York, which sought to "professionalize" philanthropy, making it capable of supporting large, ongoing projects such as libraries and universities. This type of professional philanthropy received an additional boost two years later when President Woodrow Wilson signed into law the United States Revenue Act of 1913, formally approving tax exemptions for religious, scientific, or educational purposes.

A second boost occurred after World War II, when colleges, universities, and community colleges (then often called *junior colleges*) were rapidly expanding because of the GI Bill. In order to provide the type of educational opportunities that the large new classes of students wanted and needed, schools began establishing offices devoted exclusively to fundraising. As a result, more than seventy-five public and private institutions had endowments of more than a billion dollars by the first decade of the twenty-first century.

The division of the institution that deals the most directly with fundraising may be known by a number of different names. Frequently, the office will have the terms *development, advancement,* or *community engagement* in its title. (For the purposes of this book, we'll treat these three terms as largely synonymous, although offices of community engagement sometimes deal with issues of marketing, public relations, and economic impact that are housed elsewhere at other institutions.) Although the external funding that a school receives may also involve an office of research or sponsored programs, there's a commonly accepted distinction between what that office does and the activities performed by the development staff.

Research offices are involved with projects that involve grants and contracts and that seek to provide a specific product. Development offices, on the other hand, work more extensively with gifts and endowments that don't guarantee a result, although they may sometimes commit the institution to a process. For example, if a faculty member applies for and receives a grant from the National Endowment for the Humanities (NEH) to produce a book about the history of immigrants arriving in the United States during the early twentieth century, that activity culminates in a specific product (the book) for which the grant is a type of contract; the funding will, thus, be handled by the office of research.

Indirect costs, the expenses incurred by the institution for overseeing the project (such as certain overhead costs, telephone charges, and personnel expenses for administration and security), are usually charged to the grant by the research office because these expenses result from grant activity in general rather than from any particular grant. If, however, a donor gave the school an endowment to fund a new center for immigration studies, that funding isn't contingent on the production of a specific, tangible product. Rather, it establishes a process (the activities and operation of the center) and, thus, is an appropriate matter for the development office to oversee instead of the office of grants and sponsored research.

Because this office too has overhead and other administrative costs that derive from fundraising activity in general rather than from any particular donation, it may assess a gift fee, a percentage of the contribution that is set aside to fund the school's development operations. As you can imagine, the distinction between a gift and a grant sometimes becomes blurred in actual practice, and there's a need for clear institutional procedures in order to avoid internal misunderstandings about who is in charge of which externally funded project.

Within the division of advancement, a DO may be assigned to an individual academic area (such as arts and letters, science, engineering, or business administration), particular types of fundraising (such as annual giving, major gifts, planned giving, and a capital campaign), or some combination of the two. The DO's role is to represent the interests of both the donors and the institution, making sure not only that gifts fulfill the donors' intent but also that the institution's own policies and procedures are scrupulously followed.

Good DOs can provide guidance to academic administrators that helps them adhere to acceptable standards in the field, such as those set by the Council for the Advancement and Support of Education (CASE) and the Association of Fundraising Professionals (AFP). In addition, the DO should be familiar with all applicable policies of the U.S. Internal Revenue Code (IRC) and either the Governmental Accounting Standards Board (GASB: for public institutions) or the Financial Accounting Standards Board (FASB: for private institutions).

The major sectors of the U.S. economy can be pictured as three legs of a single stool. (See Figure 1.1.) There's the *government sector* (which receives money through taxes and tariffs), the *corporate or business sector* (which receives money through the sale of goods and services), and the *nonprofit sector* (which receives money through gifts and grants). Although the source of funding is different for these three sectors, how they expend their money may be relatively similar.

Each sector pays its employees salary and benefits, has daily operating expenses, makes capital investments, and purchases the raw materials and supplies that it needs to do its job. When a recession occurs, the government is forced to curtail services, the corporate sector is forced to consider layoffs, and the nonprofit sector is forced to cut back its philanthropic activities. In the best case scenario, two of the sectors may offset damage to the entire system if, for whatever reason, the third sector is experiencing temporary setbacks. In the worst-case scenario, a death spiral occurs: The corporate sector cuts wages, which reduces tax revenue to the government and charitable giving to the nonprofits. Those two sectors then stop purchasing the goods and services of the corporate sector, and the situation rapidly deteriorates.

In addition to having different funding sources, the three sectors of the economy also differ in what they produce. For the corporate world, both sides

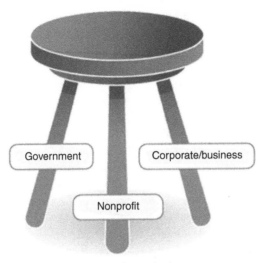

Figure 1.1   Major Sectors of Funding in the United States.

of the equation are financial: Money comes in in the form of sales and investments; it goes out to owners and investors in the form of profits.

The government and nonprofit sectors are different. Nonprofits' income may be financial, but their ultimate goal is impact, not financial gain. These two sectors are judged by their effectiveness in providing services, addressing the needs of clients, and improving programs. So, despite all the talk by legislators and governing boards that "higher education should be run more like a business," that simile only goes so far. Customers purchase products, but citizens don't purchase highways, and students don't purchase grades: They purchase access. The end result—arriving at a specific destination, whether actual or metaphorical—requires effort and commitment on the part of the person who paid the taxes or tuition. If there's a road leading to your dream vacation spot, but you never use it, it's your own fault that you didn't get there. If there's an academic program leading to your dream job, but you never study, you shouldn't blame the university for your own failure.

Understanding how the nonprofit sector is both similar to and different from other parts of the economy is essential to successful fundraising. What you're doing when you meet with a prospect is asking that person to "make an investment in higher education," but that investment isn't at all like the one a person might make if he or she were buying shares of stock in a company.

Financial investments in a company are intended to yield profits. Financial investments in a college are intended to yield social benefits. For this reason, DOs and academic administrators each play an important role in communicating what the access and impact of a proposed gift will be. For example, the DO might explain why directing a donation toward a charitable remainder annuity trust is the best type of investment for the benefactor's personal goals, whereas the academic administrator can explain why directing the income from that annuity toward scholarships is the best type of investment for the benefactor's philanthropic goals.

And make no mistake about it: The donors who have the resources to give a gift large enough to transform a program are the very same people who understand business well enough to know exactly how return on investment works. They'll have questions about the "what," "why," and "how" of each gift, and academic officers (AOs) aren't likely to be able to answer all those questions on their own. Working in collaboration with a trained DO allows you to play to your strengths, providing answers that are not only accurate but also tailored to that individual donor's goals and dreams.

There's also a second reason why successful fundraising depends on understanding how the major economic sectors relate to one another in the United States: Philanthropy itself is big business. The *Giving USA 2012 Report*, the product of an annual study by the Giving USA Foundation and the Center on Philanthropy at Indiana University, reports that Americans contributed $298.4 billion to charitable causes in 2011—$217.8 billion of which came as gifts from individual living donors, not bequests—and that those contributions were made during a period when the economy remained troubled and philanthropic activity had barely increased over the previous year, 2011. (See philanthropy.com/article/Donations-Barely-Grew-at-All/132367/.)

The *Giving USA 2013 Report* showed that $335.17 billion was in contributions with $240.60 billion in giving by individuals. Giving by bequests is expected to continue to rise with the oldest baby boomers reaching the average age of a planned gift, such as a will or trust. (See nonprofitquarterly.org/2013/06/18/giving-usa-2013-giving-coming-back-slowly-and-different-after-recession/.) In fact, the philanthropic sector of the United States is so important to the economy that recessions and changes in laws affecting nonprofits can have a ripple effect throughout the other sectors. As we saw in Figure 1.1, significant changes to any of the three legs of the U.S. economic stool can make the entire structure unstable, thus affecting individuals and communities nationwide.

So, there's also a moral imperative for academic administrators to develop strong relationships with DOs. If they truly care about the future of their programs, then they, like their donors, must make an investment in the economic health of their institutions by partnering with the development office.

For more information on what to look for when selecting a DO to work with, see Appendix A. Moreover, just as it's important for AOs to know something about how the world of fundraising works, it's also important for DOs to have some basic understanding of the organizational culture found at colleges and universities. We'll turn to that topic next. So, if you're currently a faculty member or an academic administrator, feel free to skip ahead to the next section.

A PRIMER ON ACADEMIC CULTURE FOR DEVELOPMENT PERSONNEL

Colleges, universities, and community colleges operate with a different administrative culture from that found in other organizations and even in other educational institutions, such as elementary and high schools. For one thing, they don't adhere to the rigidly hierarchical structure that one finds in corporations, military units, and many religious bodies. Those groups tend to be structured as social pyramids, with power increasing as you move up the hierarchy and the number of people at each level increasing as you move down the hierarchy. (See Figure 1.2.)

For example, there might be one chief executive officer, commander in chief, or pope; more vice presidents, generals, or cardinals; even more directors, colonels, or bishops; still more managers, lieutenants, and pastors; vastly more assistant managers, sergeants, and priests; and a huge number of employees, rank-and-file soldiers, and laity.

Organizational charts in higher education try to reproduce this structure, moving from president (or chancellor) to vice president (or vice chancellor) to dean to department chair to faculty. But colleges and universities don't really work that way. For one thing, almost everyone on the academic side of the institution holds an advanced degree and so is a specialist in an area that may not be closely related to that of his or her supervisor. A physical chemist might be the department chair of an organic chemist, and a philosopher

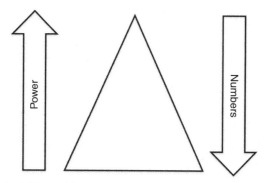

Figure 1.2 The Social Pyramid.

might be the dean of a philologist. In each case, it may initially look as though the fields of the administrator and faculty member are nearly the same but in fact they're quite different in their methods, subject matter, and historical development.

Therefore, if an organic chemist claims that the rotary evaporators in each of his or her labs must be replaced every two to three years, the chair who is a physical chemist might not know whether this request is reasonable. Similarly, if a philologist says that there's an absolute need for *L'année philologique* and the *Perseus Digital Library* to be available in every classroom where he or she teaches, the philosopher may not have the specialized knowledge to determine whether this request is appropriate.

As a result, the academic side of higher education often operates more like a community of scholars or colleagues than can be found in hierarchical organizations. Administrators are expected to trust the professional judgment of their faculty members to a far greater extent than most managers would trust the judgment of an employee when it comes to large purchases or the creation of a new product line.

It can be useful, therefore, to think of a college or university as functioning much more like a hospital than a factory, battalion, or diocese. No hospital director would dream of overturning a physician's diagnosis because the director must rely on the physician's professional expertise. That's a very different situation from what a general, an archbishop, or a corporate vice president might do when countermanding an order or decision of an underling. If hierarchical organizations function through command and control, colleges and universities place a much greater reliance on persuasion, consensus building, and group decision-making processes. That can cause their processes to seem unbearably slow at times, but it's an inherent and necessary part of how they operate.

It can be easier to understand the distinctive nature of colleges, universities, and community colleges if we view them not as social pyramids, but as distributed organizations. The most familiar type of distributed organization in the United States is the federal government. Each branch of government (legislative, judicial, and executive) has its own sphere of responsibility. (See Figure 1.3a.) That type of organization results in separation of powers. In much the same way, colleges and universities distribute power among the president and other members of the administration (policy making and implementation), the governing board (fiduciary responsibility and the hiring, evaluation, and firing of the president), and the faculty (curricular development and delivery). (See Figure 1.3b.) That type of organization results in the separation of powers dubbed *shared governance* in higher education. (See Buller, 2015, 16–18.)

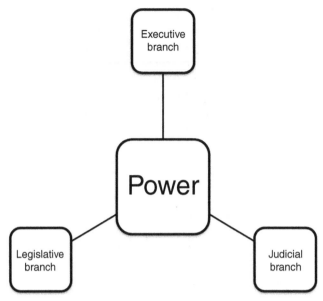

Figure 1.3a   Distributed Organization: The U.S. Federal Government.

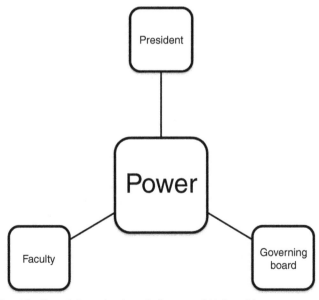

Figure 1.3b   Distributed Organization: Colleges and Universities.

Shared governance is a true separation of powers. If the president moves in a direction that the governing board does not support, it can terminate the president's contract. If the president and/or governing board move in a direction that the faculty does not support, they can refuse to develop the curriculum that is necessary to accomplish this goal and essentially veto the decision. For this reason, even though a faculty vote of no confidence in an administrator has no enforceable authority, it is always taken seriously by the institution: If the faculty aren't on board with a major initiative of a president, provost, or dean, they can keep the work of the university from being done (while still fulfilling the terms of their contracts) to such an extent that the administrator usually gives up on the initiative, resigns, or both.

It's also important to understand that as collegial and consensus based as the academic side of higher education may be, it does have its share of silos and implicit hierarchies. The silos may make communication between departments or colleges difficult. They certainly provide limits to the sphere of authority within which people operate. For example, the dean is the head of a college, but he or she really only deals with the academic aspect of work within the college. Deans can't set tuition rates by themselves, waive most fees, make commitments that would affect other segments of the institution, or resolve student housing problems.

In fact, there is a clear line delineating the areas within which a college dean and a dean of students operate. The college dean is responsible for the academic quality of a program. The dean of students is responsible for the extracurricular and cocurricular experiences of the students. So, if the negotiation for a gift is going to require permission to waive a policy, it's important that the right sort of administrator be supportive of your project. Otherwise, you may not accomplish everything that you're hoping for.

The implicit hierarchies within the academic side of a college or university may appear subtler than the rigid divisions within many corporate, military, or religious environments but they are no less real. Faculty members generally see themselves as higher in prestige than members of the staff (and, if the truth be told, than administrators). Even within the faculty ranks, tenure-track faculty members see themselves as holding higher positions than non-tenure-track faculty members. Professors often feel that their opinions take precedence over associate professors, and associate professors often feel that their opinions take precedence over assistant professors. Most of all, they regard their expertise in their disciplines as giving them preeminence in curricular matters. So, it can be unwise for either you or a donor to make suggestions about changes to what or how a faculty member teaches. Suggestions of that kind are rarely welcomed.

THE ROLE OF TRUST

Few prospects are likely to entrust a large gift to someone after a single meeting or a conversation with just one person. The donor will want to know that the project he or she is funding is important to the institution as a whole, that it's likely to continue even if the person who proposed it leaves, and that the gift will be used for the purpose it was given.

An advantage of working in groups when you meet with prospects is that a team can address these issues rather quickly. Since more than one person is involved from the very start of the discussion, it's clear that the project isn't the brainchild of just one lone individual. A group also provides a better sense of continuity since the AO is likely to be around even if the DO leaves the institution and vice versa. And the representative(s) from the development office will be able to refer to specific regulations and policies that guarantee the institution's commitment to honor the donor's intent. The result is that collaborations between the academic and the development side of the institution shorten the time it takes to gain a prospect's confidence or trust.

Trust is like a game of Shoots and Ladders: A long climb up can be followed by a rapid slide to the very bottom. By representing several facets of the institution simultaneously, collaborative approaches speed that climb while reducing the likelihood that a prospect's trust will slide before a gift agreement is complete. In addition, DOs can also help academic administrators preserve the trust of donors after a gift has been made.

There's one additional practical advantage for meeting with prospective donors as a group: Having more than one person in a meeting allows you to check whether you've understood what a prospect has said and gives you an opportunity to gather your thoughts every now and then. If an administrator meets with a prospect alone, he or she has to be "on" at every moment. When those unexpected and awkward moments arrive—and, you can count on it, they will arrive—and a donor suddenly moves the conversation in an unexpected direction, it's helpful to have someone else present who can give you time to readjust your thoughts and possibly redirect the discussion to its original focus.

For example, suppose you're a dean who's meeting with a prospect to discuss an endowment for a new scholarship. If the prospect says that he or she doesn't care about scholarships and endowments but is really more interested in talking about making a ten-year pledge of expendable money to the athletic program, you're going to need time to decide whether your role in this meeting is over or whether there's still a way to salvage your original concept. The few minutes that the DO takes to follow up on this new idea gives you time to think. And since DOs understand the many gift options that are available, they may be able to come up with ways to achieve the donor's goal and simultaneously help your program. Perhaps the donor would consider a fund that helps student athletes in your area or that provides tutoring services for athletes who are taking courses in your college. Having the DO present can, thus, give you options between insisting on your original concept and giving up entirely.

Finally, we may as well admit it: Many academic administrators simply don't like asking for money. They feel as though by doing so they're simply begging or are worried that they'll be embarrassed if the prospect says "no." Probably the greatest value in the collaborative approach for the academic administrator is that he or she doesn't have to be the one who asks for the money.

As said earlier, the advantage in being part of a development team is that you can play to your strengths. As a provost, dean, or department chair, you know your academic program inside and out. You can provide a sense of passion or excitement in describing how the gift will benefit people and why the world will be a better place as a result of this donation. When the time comes for the ask, your DO can do that work for you. At the same time, he or she will be able to answer the donor's technical questions—such as "If I endow this program, how much interest on that investment is the Foundation likely to generate?" or "How long will I have to wait until the endowment produces enough funding to implement the program completely?"—and suggest alternatives if the donor says "no" or "not" at this time. Having accurate answers readily available builds trust and makes you much more successful in your fundraising efforts.

WHAT DOs GAIN FROM COLLABORATING WITH ACADEMIC LEADERS

Just as there are many advantages of the collaborative approach for academic administrators, so do DOs benefit from this type of relationship. Working with faculty members can be difficult, even when they understand that the funding you're seeking will support an activity they regard as extremely important. It's not uncommon for college professors to believe that, as long as they argue forcefully enough for the need of a certain project, a donor will come forward and fund it in exactly the same form they envisioned. In other words, members of the faculty often stress their need for funding rather than how the donation will help the donor. They may not understand how hard it is to obtain external funding for things such as faculty salaries or conference travel.

Having an academic administrator on your team can help you bridge this gap, moving from the way in which college professors typically see the world to the way in which those outside of academia frequently see it. Together, the AO and the DO can provide a valuable educational function, teaching faculty members who are new to fundraising how to build long-term relationships with donors and how it's possible to modify proposals so that both the donor and the recipient gain something from the gift.

Moreover, just as your presence in a group can help the administrator when he or she needs a moment to think during a conversation with a prospect, so can the AO you're working with provide you with the same favor. When the prospect's questions burrow down deeply into academic areas that are not within your expertise, the administrator can take the lead in the conversation while you take a moment to collect your thoughts about where to proceed next.

Finally, even though you probably work with the faculty and administration on a daily basis, many donors still regard it as an honor to speak directly with a "real, live university dean." The collaborative approach, thus, adds a certain amount of *gravitas* to your work with donors that you may not be able to provide yourself. There are times when the administrator you're assigned to seems to complement your skills and personality immediately.

There are other times when you may need to put a lot of effort into building that highly effective type of relationship. But whether it arrives naturally or only after considerable effort, it's important to work together in a collegial and collaborative manner so as to achieve your shared goals. For more on the advantages of this approach, see the authors' companion volume, *World-Class Fundraising Isn't a Spectator Sport: The Team Approach to Academic Fundraising* (2016).

CASE STUDY

A DO with ten years of fundraising experience is working with a dean who has just begun her position at the university. Until the previous year, the dean was a highly effective department chair at a much smaller college in another state. Her current position is her first deanship, as well as her first opportunity to work at a large public university. The problem is that the dean is under a great deal of pressure from the provost to "get the college moving again" after a lengthy period of stagnation. One of the ways in which the dean is trying to meet the provost's expectations is by building the college's endowment for scholarships. Together, the dean and the DO have made more than half a dozen calls on prospects, and both feel that their work together hasn't been very effective.

The DO is convinced that, in the dean's rush to build the program, she's making the ask too soon (sometimes during the very first meeting with the prospective donor), thus alienating people who might have been more generous if they were cultivated over a longer period. The dean feels that the DO may be one of the reasons why the program has stagnated: He seems to want to do little more than socialize, have expensive lunches with the prospects, and do little to advance the process fast enough to "get the college moving again" and meet the provost's expectations.

Question: How should they handle this challenge?

Possible Strategies

One way of dealing with this situation is to work on improving communication between the academic and development sides of the institution. The two colleagues in this case study are obviously not of one mind on their goals. Although both of them are under pressure to produce results quickly from their respective supervisors, they would be far more effective if they were to set aside some time, sit down together, and have a frank discussion about their concerns. They need to be candid about the challenges they're facing, identify what they see as their goals, and develop a shared course of action to meet those goals.

The DO in this case has much more experience in building long-term relationships with prospective donors, and it might be helpful for him to review for the dean how he's been successful in securing gifts that have benefited the college in the past. Learning how long this process can take and hearing more about the steps required to obtain a large gift may be helpful to the dean. The DO should offer a plan that's specific enough to meet the dean's expectation for quick results. For example, he might outline how specific prospects are to be contacted and cultivated, what the project timeline is likely to be, and what each of them can contribute to the overall effort. Then, the dean and the DO can jointly decide how best to proceed and when the appropriate time will arrive for each ask. The dean might also consider attending a workshop that offers some introductory fundraising training for academic leaders in order to have a better understanding of the advancement process.

It's impossible to establish trust with a donor if the team members don't have trust in one another. And that's something that's sorely lacking in the situation outlined here. This relationship is new, and both parties are still feeling their way toward an optimal method of working together. If they are traveling by car separately to meet with prospective donors, they could benefit from riding together and using that time to clarify their expectations of one another. If the DO has been cultivating a prospect who will soon be ready for an ask, it may be helpful to make that activity a priority.

After achieving one gift successfully, the dean may be able to relax a bit and understand that the DO really does know his job. Moreover, since the dean is new to fundraising, it may be helpful for the two of them to engage in some training jointly in order to tighten their bonds as a unit and (discreetly) provide this novice dean with the coaching she needs.

Pairs of administrators and DOs sometimes gel immediately, sometimes require a longer period to appreciate each other's strengths, and sometimes never click. But before deciding that there's something irreparably problematic about this relationship, both of them owe it to their university to explore other options of clarifying how they intend to work together and what their mutual priorities should be.

CONCLUDING THOUGHTS

Many situations in academic fundraising take people outside their comfort zone. Academic administrators may feel uneasy asking people for money and answering technical questions about the booking and use of gifts. DOs may not be comfortable making promises on behalf of a certain academic program or dealing with the jargon of a discipline they've never studied in depth. And prospective donors may be uncertain about pledging funds they worked hard to accumulate to people they know only casually and about whose motives they are unsure. Establishing trust takes time, but it also takes one other critical component: commitment to ethical principles that are accepted through the entire sphere of academic fundraising. And those principles will be the subject of Chapter 2.

REFERENCES

Buller, J. L. (2015). *Change leadership in higher education: A practical guide to academic transformation.* San Francisco, CA: Jossey-Bass.

Buller, J. L., & Reeves, D. M. (2016). *World-class fundraising isn't a spectator sport: The team approach to academic fundraising.* Lanham, MD: Rowman and Littlefield.

McAlexander, J. H., Koenig, H. F., & DuFault, B. (2014). Advancement in higher education: The role of marketing in building philanthropic giving. *Journal of Marketing for Higher Education.* (24) 2, 243–256.

RESOURCES

Alexander, G. D., & Carlson, K. J. (2005). *Essential principles for fundraising success: An answer manual for the everyday challenges of raising money.* San Francisco, CA: Jossey-Bass.

Carlson, M., & Clarke, C. (2000). *Team-based fundraising step by step: A practical guide to improving results through teamwork.* San Francisco, CA: Jossey-Bass.

Hodson, J. B. (March 2010). Leading the way: The role of presidents and academic deans in fundraising. *New Directions for Higher Education.* 149, 39–49.

Hunt, P. C. (2012). *Development for academic leaders: A practical guide for fundraising success.* San Francisco, CA: Jossey-Bass.

Thompson, K. A., & Jennings, K. N. (2009). *More than a thank you note: Academic library fundraising for the dean or director.* Oxford: Chandos.

Chapter Two

Ethical Issues in Fundraising

In Chapter 1, we saw that the role of trust is so important when it comes to fundraising that, once trust is lost, it takes a long time for development efforts to recover—if they ever do. Fundraisers earn the trust of donors in the same way that it's earned in personal relationships and corporate environments: by adhering to expected standards of behavior, keeping their word, and not treating people as though they're merely a means to an end. (On the relationship between trust and ethics, see Rosen, 2005.)

In development work, these standards are outlined in two important policy statements issued by the Association of Fundraising Professionals (AFP): the Code of Ethical Standards (sometimes also known as the Code of Ethical Standards and Principles) and the Donor Bill of Rights. (Additional electronic sources outlining principles in ethical fundraising may be found in Grobman, 2000.)

The Code of Ethical Standards (see Appendix B) outlines twenty-five principles of ethical practice, covering a wide range of fundraising activities, such as the fiduciary responsibilities of boards and fundraisers, expectations for documenting and reporting gifts, and how gifts should be valued. In the AFP's long version of these standards, each principle is accompanied by specific guidelines, as well as by examples of both ethical and unethical practices. (See www.afpnet.org/files/ContentDocuments/CodeofEthicsLong.pdf.)

The Donor Bill of Rights (see Appendix C) outlines ten basic rights that fundraising organizations should extend to each donor, such as the ability to examine the organization's most recent financial statements and to have access to information about whether the person making the solicitation is a volunteer or paid employee.

Successful academic fundraisers not only adhere to the standards outlined in the Code of Ethical Standards and the Donor Bill of Rights but also use

23

them in their ongoing training. Since ethical issues are often best understood in the context of specific situations, this chapter uses brief case studies to examine some of the most important standards found in the AFP Code of Ethical Standards and then explores the issues involved in each case. Although all of the standards are relevant to academic fundraisers, we've selected seven that are the most crucial if you want to be successful at going for the gold.

STANDARD NO. 2: MEMBERS SHALL NOT ENGAGE IN ACTIVITIES THAT CONFLICT WITH THEIR FIDUCIARY, ETHICAL, AND LEGAL OBLIGATIONS TO THEIR ORGANIZATIONS AND THEIR CLIENTS.

Case Study: Dr. Generous, a long-retired university professor without any surviving family members, wants to leave his estate to a college so that it can create a new program related to his interest in philosophy. He meets with the dean of the college, that college's development officer (DO), and the admission director to clarify what his goals are and how he'd like them to be pursued. Everyone from the college agreed that the program was relevant to the mission of the college, but they felt uncertain about the school's ability to support the full range of programming envisioned by Dr. Generous from the proceeds of the estate.

Nevertheless, the DO assured Dr. Generous that a simple will would provide enough legal direction to ensure that his wishes would be followed after he died and that she would provide him with some sample language that he could include as a codicil to his will.

Questions: Did the institution violate accepted ethical standards in this case? If so, which principles were involved? If not, how did its actions address AFP Standard No. 2?

Discussion: The college is probably in violation of AFP Standard No. 2. To begin with, Dr. Generous should have been instructed—even strongly urged—to seek his own legal counsel who would represent only the donor's interest. Although it's perfectly acceptable to provide a prospective donor with some sample language for a bequest, the DO who provides that language is inevitably representing the interests of the college.

Any well-trained DO will, of course, be aware of common philanthropic practices, but he or she can't provide genuine legal representation to the donor. In this same vein, the DO can't assure Dr. Generous that the sample language provided will cover all his intentions and can't present her advice as official legal counsel. At best, the case study presents a troubling conflict of interest. At worst, it could result in a bequest that could be subject to a legal challenge later. In fact, this case study also crosses over into the next standard that we'll consider.

STANDARD NO. 3: MEMBERS SHALL EFFECTIVELY DISCLOSE ALL POTENTIAL AND ACTUAL CONFLICTS OF INTEREST; SUCH DISCLOSURE DOES NOT PRECLUDE OR IMPLY ETHICAL IMPROPRIETY.

Case Study A: Mrs. Retiree has become a very committed supporter of Underfunded State University. Her granddaughter will be visiting her for the summer and would like to continue her music lessons. It just so happens that the dean's son is a music teacher in the area. The dean mentions to the donor that she's aware of an excellent music teacher in the area and provides the name and telephone number of her son so that the donor can initiate the contact.

Question A: Did the dean violate AFP Standard No. 3?

Discussion A: Because a member of the dean's family stands to benefit financially and professionally from this relationship, the dean did act in a way that could be viewed as ethically questionable. To be sure, situations of this nature are bound to occur, and the dean's son may, in fact, be the best possible teacher for Mrs. Retiree's daughter. Passing on contact information in this way doesn't in and of itself violate any ethical standards. But what the dean needs to do is reveal that the teacher she's recommending is her own son. Failure to do so places the dean in a situation that's questionable at best.

Case Study B: A faculty member at the university has partnered with a donor, both of whom have worked tirelessly for many years on a social project in the community. In addition to supporting this community social project, the donor has also been a major financial supporter of the university where the faculty member works. A number of the professor's students still volunteer at the organization created to support the community project, and a few of them have even taken jobs there after their graduation. The faculty member meets a number of times per year with the donor without sharing with his chair or dean the substance of most of those meetings.

In addition, although a number of possible additional contributions to the faculty member's program have been discussed in these meetings, the DO assigned to the faculty member's program is never told that these meetings are taking place. The DO does take several administrators from the school to meet with this donor from time to time, but the donor states that he "doesn't like meetings and doesn't feel a need to get together too officially or too often."

In any case, whenever these conversations occur, the DO always follows them with a note of thanks. When the donor does make a contribution, a letter of acknowledgement is always sent. But the DO always assumes that these gifts are being made randomly with no real involvement from anyone at the institution. At one point, however, when the DO is checking in with the donor by phone, the donor happens to mention that he's named the faculty member a beneficiary in his estate plan and the donor hopes that the faculty member will continue to support his philanthropic interests.

Question B: Has any ethical standard been violated? If so, at what point in the case did that violation occur? If not, how are the actions of everyone in this scenario in accordance with AFP Standard No. 3?

Discussion B: This situation is interesting in that, although it's not illegal for the faculty member to be a beneficiary of a donor's estate, the whole arrangement does carry the appearance of impropriety. In this case, the faculty member should have suggested that the donor make a gift to the nonprofit organization that supports the community project or create a new trust (with independent professional counsel), but without making the faculty member himself a beneficiary.

If, despite this advice, the donor proceeded by naming the faculty member a beneficiary, either the donor or the faculty member should have notified appropriate parties at the institution so that this relationship could be docu-mented. Since the DO found out about this arrangement inadvertently during a telephone call, it's now incumbent upon her to discuss the matter with the faculty member's supervisor as well as her own. A review would then need to be conducted by the institution's legal counsel so that the school could decide how to proceed with the relationship under the umbrella of the institution's mission and strategic plan. There's also a need to document this relationship in whatever database the school uses for fundraising purposes.

STANDARD NO. 4: MEMBERS SHALL NOT EXPLOIT ANY RELATIONSHIP WITH A DONOR, PROSPECT, VOLUNTEER, OR EMPLOYEE FOR THE BENEFIT OF THE MEMBER OR THE MEMBER'S ORGANIZATION.

Case Study A: A dean, DO, marketing director, and chair of the alumni board are working together to manage a development council that supports one of the colleges at a university. As part of the council's regular meetings, a small group of students and faculty members speak for a few minutes about their academic interests, current activities, and future plans.

One day, a member of this council approaches the dean to complain that one of the professors who spoke to the group has been contacting him repeatedly, pressuring him for tickets to professional football games, since the head coach of the local team is close friends with the council member. The council member had offered some tickets to this faculty member once in the past when he was unable to use them, but he now feels uncomfortable because of the professor's frequent and insistent requests. He wonders whether he should resign from the council so that he can avoid confronting the professor.

Question A: Did the institution violate AFP Standard No. 4?

Discussion A: Even though the professor isn't a member of the AFP, the institution is, and its employees are, thus, expected to adhere to its standards. Although it'll be uncomfortable to do so, the dean should discuss this matter with the faculty member and make it clear that such a request can never recur.

Many times, supporters of an institution offer tickets they're not intending to use in the hope that someone associated with a cause they care about will benefit from their generosity. But when the situation isn't one of making a gift but rather of being confronted with a request or demand, it's a reasonable conclusion that the faculty member is exploiting his or her relationship with the council.

One idea for the future might be for council members to provide gifts such as the football tickets to the university in general so that an appropriate committee or administrative office can establish a process for fair distribution to those who work at the institution. The recipient would then be encouraged to write a note of appreciation or, if the gift is particularly large, make a donation to the university in the benefactor's name. Doing so would reinforce the notion that the interaction wasn't really between a council member and a faculty member but concerned both of their relationships with the institution.

Case Study B: A member of a college's fundraising council works as a wealth manager at a local investment firm. Over a period, this council member has approached a number of other people on the board, particularly those with a high net worth, and tried to recruit them as clients. In addition, this council member's husband is the executive director of another nonprofit organization in the area. At college events, he accompanies her and "works the room" as if it were his own organization's event. Several members have complained to the administration about this practice and expressed their annoyance about having to state repeatedly that they are not interested in giving her their business or supporting her husband's organization. They're now asking the dean and DO to do something to stop this aggressive behavior.

Question B: Has anyone in this scenario violated AFP Standard No. 4?

Discussion B: As this case study suggests, exploiting relationships can work both ways when it comes to donors and employees of a college or university. A good approach might be for the chair of the fundraising council to include a discussion of APF standards at its orientation meetings for new members and then to reinforce these standards during regular board training. Since the topic is sensitive, it's probably best addressed as a general principle rather than by singling out any particular council member. Even so, in the current case where multiple complaints are being made, the dean and/or DO should probably meet with the council member and have a candid discussion about this issue.

Nevertheless, if the board were a true governing board, as opposed to an advisory or a fundraising board, the problem would be far more serious and probably require the intervention of the president and perhaps even the termination of the offending member from the board.

STANDARD NO. 10: MEMBERS SHALL PROTECT THE CONFIDENTIALITY OF ALL PRIVILEGED INFORMATION RELATING TO THE PROVIDER/CLIENT RELATIONSHIPS.

Case Study: A university president, her DO, and the vice president for business affairs are having lunch with a prospect they've been cultivating for more than a year, hoping to receive a leadership gift that will benefit the university's new medical school. Over the course of lunch, the prospect is talking about his contacts who might be approached to join with him in making a major gift. In particular, he names a certain Mr. Croesus who's known to support projects in the health sciences and who recently gave $20 million to a medical program at his alma mater. Neither the president nor the DO was aware that a member of their own community had made this gift, because, although Mr. Croesus had told the prospect who was a close friend, he had asked his school to list him only as an anonymous donor.

As the lunch continues, the prospective donor shifts the conversation and asks the president about one of her most important financial supporters, Ms. Affluent, after whom the medical school is going to be named. Since the amount of Ms. Affluent's gift was never publicized, the prospect's line of questioning is unsettling to the president: "Naming an entire school must cost a pretty penny. How much did *that* set her back?" It's unclear whether the prospect is asking the question out of idle curiosity or to determine what range of gift might be expected of him and Mr. Croesus.

Question: Would the president be wrong to answer the question?

Discussion: Although the prospect may have revealed information about Mr. Croesus that he shouldn't have, it's incumbent upon others involved in academic fundraising not to make a similar mistake. If the value of naming rights at the institution is disseminated publicly, it's perfectly acceptable to refer to this general policy. But the president and DO should refrain from sharing the actual gift amount. One possible response might be, "Oh, well, Ms. Affluent has always been rather private about the gifts she so generously makes to the University, and we'd certainly like to maintain the confidentiality she has requested, just as we would do for every donor unless that person specifies otherwise. But what I can say is that naming rights for our academic programs start in the range of $30 million and increase according to the size and complexity of the program."

STANDARD NO. 13: MEMBERS SHALL TAKE CARE TO ENSURE THAT DONORS RECEIVE INFORMED, ACCURATE, AND ETHICAL ADVICE ABOUT THE VALUE AND TAX IMPLICATIONS OF CONTRIBUTIONS.

Case Study: Beneficent Griever travels across the country to take care of her deceased father's estate. In addition to handling all the financial and legal issues, Ms. Griever had to dispose of his material goods, out of which she chose to take only a few personal items to which she was sentimentally attached. What remained included a large amount of furniture, electronic equipment, appliances, and works of art. She knew that her father enjoyed his involvement with a college near where he lived, and she called that institution to see whether it could use some of these items. The DO agreed to meet her, and Ms. Griever took her on a quick tour of her father's home.

As they walked through the house together, the DO agreed that some of the appliances and electronic equipment might be useful to the college, and Ms. Griever was happy to arrange to have them delivered. She then asked the DO whether any of the artwork was useful to them, since she didn't share the same tastes as her father and didn't think it was worth much anyway, certainly no more than $200. When the DO examined the art, she realized something that a person from across the country probably wouldn't have known: It included a series by a local landscape artist from the 1950s whose works were becoming increasingly popular and valuable. The DO readily agreed to take the paintings off the daughter's hands and said she'd send a receipt for the amount the daughter had said the paintings were worth to her.

The DO later told her supervisor about the smart move she'd made since the daughter was delighted to receive a tax deduction and to be rid of the paintings, whereas the college could sell them for a sizable amount. "It's a win-win situation," she said, "Everyone benefits, and no one was hurt."

Question: Is the DO right?

Discussion: This case actually involves not just one but two major ethical violations: The DO withheld information about the value of the items that were donated, and the DO specified the value of the items for tax purposes.

The first thing the DO should have done was to inform the daughter about what she knew of the works' potential value and to have allowed her to make a more informed decision. Her willingness to conceal information is ethically no different from lying and could leave the college liable to legal actions as a result.

Additionally, receipts that state the value of noncash contributions for tax benefits can only be prepared by a professional appraiser unless the items are publicly traded commodities with a value that can easily be verified. In the event that the daughter still wished to donate the artwork after she knew its history and potential value, all that information should be recorded in writing and accompanied by photographs of the paintings themselves. Even if the increased value was determined only after the donation, the daughter should have still been notified and given the option of rescinding the gift, less any cost was incurred by the college to verify the value of the donation.

This ethical breach is serious enough that the DO could face termination for cause if her supervisor pursues the matter. AFT Standard No. 13 highlights the importance of providing a statement of fair market value for any services or goods received in exchange for contributions. Although the violation described in the scenario is particularly egregious, academic leaders and DOs encounter a similar, but far more subtle challenge when they issue tickets for institutionally sponsored events.

If the cost of the ticket includes a donation, the amount of the ticket that was used to pay for the activity itself (such as a dinner or gala) must be clearly distinguished from the tax-deductible portion of the ticket price. A disclaimer on the invitation itself serves as protection for both the donor (who will know how much to record as a contribution for tax purposes) and the organization (which cannot then be accused of trying to mislead the contributors).

For instance, if it costs an institution $100 per person to conduct an event, and the ticket price is $300, the invitation and/or ticket will usually include a statement saying something like, "contributions in excess of $100 per person may be tax deductible as permitted by law." The Internal Revenue Service document *Charitable Contributions: Substantiation and Disclosure Requirements* (Publication 1771) outlines the substantiation and disclosure requirements for nonprofits. Among the rules outlined in that document are the following:

> A donor is responsible for obtaining a written acknowledgement from a charity for any single contribution of $250 or more before the donor can claim a charitable contribution on his/her federal income tax return. A charitable organization is required to provide a written disclosure to a donor who receives goods or services in exchange for a single payment in excess of $75. irs.gov/pub/irs-pdf/p1771.pdf

The Internal Revenue Service also provides additional information about these policies on its website.

STANDARD NO. 14: MEMBERS SHALL TAKE CARE TO ENSURE THAT CONTRIBUTIONS ARE USED IN ACCORDANCE WITH DONORS' INTENTIONS.

Case Study: A donor endows a fund to support an annual event at a university. The fund covers the costs needed to bring in a guest speaker in the social sciences, including an honorarium, travel, meals, and accommodations. The event is in its seventh year when the donor dies without leaving heirs. Three years later, the chair of the Department of Sociology, who is planning the event that year, decides independently to "tweak" the use of the funds. Under his plan, the public event would still be held every other year, but in the intervening years revenue from the fund would be used to support faculty members in the social sciences who want to present their research at conferences. "There really is no problem," the chair argues, "We're still using the fund for the donor's intent. We're continuing to expand awareness of research done in our field, and we're doing so by covering travel, meal, and lodging expenses. We're just shifting use of the fund slightly in light of our most pressing needs."

Question: Is the chair correct?

Discussion: Adjustments of this sort are among the most common proposals made by faculty members and academic administrators to DOs. What the school will need to do is to examine the parameters established in the original gift agreement to determine how flexible they were and whether any provision was made for using the funds differently if needs changed. The intended purpose of a gift can't be altered frivolously or arbitrarily by any individual. In this case, if the gift agreement specifically states that the funds are to be used to bring guest speakers to the campus, they can't be diverted to faculty travel. In the event that there are remaining family members who've been designated as contacts for the fund, they could be consulted about the proposed change. But that isn't the case in the situation described earlier. (At least, it doesn't appear to be the case since the donor had no heirs.) If living relatives of the donor are found, however, a written addendum to the original agreement could be prepared and signed by them, allowing the funds to be used for the new purpose.

In the event that a program is discontinued since it's no longer relevant to the college's mission or is no longer needed, the fund may be reevaluated to determine the most proper use of the funds. Under the doctrine of *cy-près* (a French term meaning "as close as possible"), legal counsel can help determine whether the continued use of the funds as originally intended by the donor would be impracticable or illegal. Any review and approval of a change in the use of funds require that the general intent of the donor must be observed as closely as possible.

For example, suppose that the institution were state supported, and the state legislature decided to fund every single guest speaker any academic program wanted to bring to campus. (Yes, we know how improbable that scenario is, but bear with us for a moment.) In that case, the donor's gift would no longer be needed for its original purpose and could be applied to the closest possible need the institution still had.

One of the few exceptions that allows schools to change the use of restricted funds is addressed by the Uniform Prudent Management of Institutional Funds Act (UPMIFA, available at uniformlaws.org/shared/docs/ prudent%20mgt%20of%20institutional%20funds/upmifa_final_06.pdf). This act, adopted in 2007, helped establish a more consistent set of investment policies related to charitable funds. One section of the UPMIFA states that a fund with a value of less than $25,000 that has been in place for more than twenty years doesn't require court action if the charity determines that a restriction on how the beneficiary may expend the funds is "unlawful, impracticable, impossible to achieve, or wasteful."

In order to take advantage of this provision, the organization must wait sixty days after giving notice of its intent to the State Attorney General, arguing that the change is designed to be a more appropriate way of fulfilling the donor's expressed charitable purposes. Most states in the United States have adopted UPMIFA, although some states have modified the maximum threshold of $25,000 to meet more appropriate local financial standards.

Several AFP standards specifically address the use of funds and the intention of the donor. The AFP recommends that organizations properly document philanthropic contributions in such a way that the following items are all specifically addressed:

- the gift amount
- the payment schedule
- the donor's philanthropic intention and expectations
- the schedule on which stewardship reports will be made, describing how the funds were used and what outcomes, if any, were achieved

Most colleges and universities have templates that can be used for gifts that are expendable, endowed, or program related. These templates provide a level of assurance that the AFP standards are being followed and that the donor's intention is respected.

*STANDARD NO. 21: MEMBERS SHALL NOT ACCEPT
COMPENSATION OR ENTER INTO A CONTRACT THAT
IS BASED ON A PERCENTAGE OF CONTRIBUTIONS;
NOR SHALL MEMBERS ACCEPT FINDER'S FEES OR
CONTINGENT FEES. BUSINESS MEMBERS MUST
REFRAIN FROM RECEIVING COMPENSATION FROM
THIRD PARTIES DERIVED FROM PRODUCTS OR
SERVICES FOR A CLIENT WITHOUT DISCLOSING THAT
THIRD-PARTY COMPENSATION TO THE CLIENT.*

Case Study: The head of a new graduate research program happened to run into an old friend who had a number of important connections in the field. The program head persistently asked his friend to help him raise money for the program even though she had never worked as a fundraiser before. When she finally agreed to help (after much cajoling and persuasion), the program director offered her a job on his staff. He said he couldn't pay her a salary, since start-up funding for the program was meager, but that he'd pay her a commission based on how much she raised.

"For example, if you bring in less than $500,000," he said, "I'll pay you 5% of what you raise. That percentage will go up for each $500,000 up to $5 million. So, say you raise $750,000, you'd get 5.25% of that. Raise $4 million, and you'll get 6%. $5 million or more: 6.5%. Plus, for every new donor at the $5,000 level or higher, I'll pay you an extra $500. Sound fair?"

Since his friend was a novice without any professional fundraising training or experience, she agreed. The program head was delighted with his clever plan. But when he told the vice president of advancement about this entrepreneurial new contract he'd negotiated, the VP was livid.

Question: Why was the vice president so upset about an arrangement that seemed to help everyone and harm no one?

Discussion: The reason why ethical standards prevent fundraisers from receiving commissions on the money they raise is that this system can easily taint the fundraiser's motives in seeking a donation. Since what the person earns is tied to how much he or she raises, there is an incentive to raise money in a way that benefits the fundraiser, not the mission of the organization or the philanthropic goals of the donors.

For example, the program director's friend could be under a strong temptation to skew her presentation of the project to a donor in such a way as to be misleading or even overtly dishonest.

AFP Standard No. 21 illustrates why it's inadvisable to engage in academic fundraising on your own: Working closely with others can keep you and your organization out of trouble. With one or more members of the group always having substantial development training, there will be someone ready at hand during discussions of approaches such as the one in this scenario to explain why commission-based fundraising is unethical. (And in our experience, rarely a year goes by at a college or university when someone doesn't suggest this idea.) The availability of a well-trained DO can help guide conversations toward a more constructive direction when someone's "brilliant new idea" threatens to introduce an ethically questionable practice.

ETHICS QUERIES

Membership in the AFP is voluntary for both individuals and organizations. Nevertheless, colleges, universities, and community colleges generally uphold principles similar to those outlined in the AFP standards. Moreover, an ethics query or complaint may be filed by anyone who believes that the AFP Code of Ethical Principles and Standards has been violated. That process can begin by letter, fax, or telephone call, directed as follows:

Association of Fundraising Professionals
4300 Wilson Blvd., Suite 300
Arlington, VA 22203
Phone: 703-684-0410
Toll free: 800-666-3863
Fax: 703-684-0540
www.afpnet.org

The AFP also has an online Ethical Assessment Inventory that members can use to evaluate their current practices in light of best practices in the field.

TEN QUESTIONS FOR MAKING ETHICAL DECISIONS IN FUNDRAISING

As a way of providing a more immediate evaluation of a situation that you may regard as ethically questionable, here are ten questions that academic fundraisers can ask themselves to determine whether or not to proceed in a given direction.

1. If this action resulted in publicity "above the fold" on the first page of a local newspaper (or on the main page of a news website) or in *The Chronicle of Higher Education*, would it be viewed favorably or unfavorably?

2. Would this decision support or divert the mission of the organization?
3. Would this choice maintain and build or detract from trust you've built with the donor and/or general public?
4. Would this action be perceived as a short-term gain that could prevent a long-term advance for the college/organization?
5. Would this action make you personally feel comfortable or uncomfortable?
6. Even if your legal representatives declare that nothing in the law would prevent you from taking this course of action, is there anything about it that you believe is morally questionable or indefensible in terms of your core values?
7. Are all parties to this decision being treated with dignity and respect?
8. Are conflicts of interest and even perceived conflicts of interest avoided by this course of action?
9. Does this action meet expected standards of behavior in higher education?
10. Has this course of action been vetted at all appropriate levels of the institution?

Although the world often seems ambiguous with regard to certain ethical choices, successful academic fundraisers always strive to adhere to the highest levels of practice with regard to fundraising ethics. Part of what makes a well-organized development office successful is that it supports the mission of the institution in a legal, morally defensible, and transparent manner. A single misstep that ruins the reputation of a person or an organization may cause irreparable damage. Taking the time to be methodical and make decisions you can readily justify is simply sound practice.

ETHICAL MOVES MANAGEMENT

Much of academic fundraising appears inherently goal oriented: What's the best way to support this new program, construct this new building, endow this new faculty line, or accomplish whatever financial goal the institution has? As a result, it can be tempting at times to adopt a whatever-it-takes strategy to reach a goal, using the ends to justify the means. World-class academic fundraisers understand, however, that this approach is extremely shortsighted. Treating prospective donors with respect and dignity not only makes good ethical sense but also makes good fundraising sense. That's why fundraisers who have an institution's best interests in mind engage in ethical moves management.

Moves management is a future-oriented and intentional process of assisting a prospect in his or her development from potential donor to actual donor and/ or from donor at a lower level to donor at a higher level of giving. We might think of moves management as combining strategic and tactical planning with gap analysis in the area of donor cultivation. At its core, this process is based on three fundamental questions:

1. How might we define our current relationship with each of our external constituents (i.e., friends, supporters, potential donors, and donors)?
2. As realistically as possible, what would we like that relationship to be?
3. What are the steps that could take this constituent from #1 to #2?

In other words, moves management identifies the distance between where our donors are right now and where we reasonably would like them to be (i.e., the "gap") and then develops a workable method to bridge that gap (i.e., the strategic and tactical plan).

When a group of academic fundraisers meets for the purpose of discussing moves management, it considers issues such as how to get people who support the basic mission of an academic program to attend more of its events, those who attend its events to make regular contributions to its annual fund, those who make regular contributions to the annual fund to pledge at a higher level, those who pledge at a high level to consider a major gift, and those who contribute major gifts to leave a legacy.

At the same time, it may involve recognizing that certain people, though they can always be counted on to attend institutional events and help raise awareness of the school's activities in the community, are simply unwilling or unable to provide financial resources to your program. Continuing to solicit them for a contribution is, thus, counterproductive: It alienates someone who was once a strong community supporter while not helping the institution financially.

In a similar way, moves management meetings help you decide when it's time to stop calling on a prospect who's always happy to be taken out to lunch or dinner but who never contributes at a level that makes those meals worthwhile.

Although any fundraising approach involves identifying prospective donors who can be cultivated for an initial gift or increasing their level of giving, the difference that moves management brings to this process is the systematic way in which this effort is conducted.

As Harvey Mackay noted in a statement he attributes to an anonymous friend, "A dream is just a dream. A goal is a dream with a plan and a deadline." (Mackay, 1988, 78) What moves management does is to add the plan and the timetable to your hopes and dreams. It means that, on some fixed schedule (perhaps weekly, perhaps semimonthly), representatives of the college or university systematically go through their list of prospects, identify their next goal for each prospect, and review the specific steps that various members have taken toward reaching that goal since the previous moves meeting. The result of one of these meetings may look something like the following:

- Prospect A: Currently contributes $100 a year to the program. Goal is $1,000 a year. Sent personal invitation to this week's guest lecture.
- Prospect B: Contributed $100,000 to scholarship fund three years ago. Goal is a second, similar gift. Casual lunch with dean and eminent scholar set for Thursday.
- Prospect C: Provides $10,000 annually to scholarship fund. Has clearly stated unwillingness to increase gift (due to other philanthropic priorities) and dislike of frequent solicitation. Strategy: Let prospect lie fallow for now.
- Prospect D: Frequent attendance at institutional events, but no gift to date. Letter proposing small initial gift to annual fund will be sent next week. If no response, remove from active prospect list for one year.
- Prospect E: Steady annual fund gifts of $1,000 or more each year for fourteen years. Department chair will discuss possibility of $10,000 gift in area of prospect's choice within two weeks.

The idea is, thus, to incorporate cultivation, stewardship, good community relations, and targeted planning into an overall strategy for improving the institution's access to external sources of funding.

What makes an approach to this process world class, however, is a consistent focus on ethical ways of proceeding rather than merely effective ways of proceeding. It gives serious attention to the ways in which the institution can help a donor achieve his or her own philanthropic goals. Fundraisers don't act like unscrupulous salesmen who are trying to make a client purchase something that he or she really doesn't want.

Successful academic fundraising looks, therefore, for clear areas of overlap between the school's own goals and the donor's interests. If someone from the institution begins speaking in terms of talking the donor into something, other members of the development team feel empowered enough to intervene and redirect the conversation toward more appropriate lines of proceeding.

CASE STUDY

The DO's heart was pounding. The moment felt more than simply awkward. The 5'2" potential donor didn't sit down after she and the dean entered his office. The DO herself had always been considered tall, and the dean who accompanied her was 6'6" in height, but both felt small as the prospect stared at them, unblinking and unsmiling. They were trying to explain that, even though the chancellor had said she'd join them, something unavoidable had arisen on campus, and so the meeting would be with just them.

The DO stumbled over her words. "Well, you see, since we were almost here, we thought we'd go ahead and talk with you about our ideas. Perhaps we can arrange for you to meet with the chancellor some time. In that way . . ."

"Let's get one thing straight," the potential donor interrupted without a trace of friendliness in his voice, "There will be no more meetings. What I'm going to tell you today is that there will be no money from me for anything that involves your university, and there will still be no money if she ever does do me the courtesy to show up. So, why waste our time?" He stood up, rested his fists on his desk, and stared directly at the DO.

The initial reaction was for the dean and the DO to cut their losses, apologize, thank him for his time, and bolt for the door. But the DO knew that this potential donor had, indeed, given several large gifts to the university earlier and had already expressed interest in the very same Alzheimer's research project they'd come there to discuss. It was possible that he'd even regret it later if the project took place without his involvement. As she stood there, she felt faced, not just with a development challenge but with a real ethical problem: What was the best thing to do?

QUESTIONS

1. In light of the potential donor's words and demeanor, which of the following seems the best alternative for the DO and dean?
   a. Stick with their original impulses, apologize, and leave.
   →b. Leave as graciously as possible but follow up later with a further apology and an attempt to reconnect.
   c. Try to salvage the situation and present their ideas, hoping that the prospect's attitude would change when he learned that their project was something he'd earlier expressed interest in.
   d. Simply ignore the prospective donor's gruff remarks and proceed anyway, assuming that they had nothing to lose and much to gain from being persistent.
   e. Do something else.
2. If the group decides to proceed, either immediately or at a later date, is it violating ethical principles by trying to talk the prospective donor into something he'd said he wouldn't help fund?
3. What is the most ethical way of salvaging this already very difficult situation? What's the best outcome the institution can hope for?

CASE STUDY OUTCOME

The DO took a deep breath and waited. The donor went on about how he did not have any funds to direct to any more causes and how he felt taken advantage of by people like the two of them. "Everyone and his brother approaches me with a hand out. That happened occasionally before, but it's almost daily now that Sylvia [his wife] and I were named philanthropists of the year last year. Look, I know your chancellor from the Chamber of Commerce, and I already told her that I'm not giving another dime to your university. You've already picked my pocket, and now it's time for me to give my ten million dollars a year to other causes that are important to me."

For the next few minutes, the prospective donor ranted about people who approached him only to use him and how tired he was of the constant solicitations. But the DO noticed that, as he continued talking, his tone gradually softened. His anger appeared to be burning itself out, and he ended on an almost apologetic note. "I don't mean to take all of this out on you. You're only doing your job. And your university is doing some really great things. I'm happy that I was able to support it in the past, and I think it was a good investment. But now I'm just overwhelmed by the number of causes people expect me to support."

When there finally was a break in the prospective donor's monologue, the dean spoke up with a conciliatory message. "We really do understand completely. You do a lot of good things for the community, and you've done a lot of good things for the university. Sure, we'd love to have a building for our new Alzheimer's research project bearing your name, but we respect your position and don't want to press you on it."

As the dean was speaking, an old fundraising adage came to the DO. (See Textbox 2.1.)

> *If you want money, ask for advice; if you want advice, ask for money.*

She smiled at the prospective donor and said, "Since we really do need that building for our project to succeed, though, can you tell us a bit about how we could do a better job getting people to support it? Really, any help you could give us—the right people to contact, the right questions to ask, the right time to reach out to people—would be very much appreciated. We just want to do this right."

The prospective donor shrugged and said that everyone was doing the same thing; they certainly didn't need his advice. But then he launched into another long monologue. He talked about one project he had funded related to Alzheimer's research. Then another. And then another. He laid out detail after detail about all these pet projects. After nearly twenty minutes had gone by, the dean followed the DO's lead and said, "Well, it sounds as though we have a lot of overlapping interests. And I'm sure you really can help us by giving us some insights into what made you want to contribute to those projects. How did people approach you with the idea? Or did you approach them? What did you want to know before you agreed to help?"

The prospective donor talked a little bit more about why he chose the projects that he did, and finally the dean and DO could tell the meeting was winding down. In closing, they asked the prospective donor whether he could be considered a friend of the university and whether they could keep him on the mailing list for information about the Alzheimer's project as it developed. They asked him to keep them in mind if he ever thought of someone who might be willing to purchase the naming rights for the building. The prospective donor agreed, and the two visitors reached for their business cards so that they could leave them with their host.

"Oh, no!" the prospective donor chuckled. "I've got plenty of your cards already!" As he offered to see them out of the building, he started sharing the history of his business and his family involvement. It was nearly half an hour later before they finally reached their car. As he left them, the prospective donor said, "I know your Alzheimer's project's going to be successful. You have a good program, and you're persistent; I'll grant you that. You'll do just fine."

CASE STUDY DISCUSSION

There are certain situations when fundraising goals, ethical issues, and sheer human decency all come together. This case study is one of those situations. If the donor had not previously expressed any interest or given any support to Alzheimer's research, the team members probably would have been justified in trusting their first instincts and cutting the meeting short. But because of the donor's previous history, the situation became a bit more complex: Was his initially dismissive response really due to an unwillingness to consider further solicitations, a reaction to the chancellor's failure to show up, the result of a bad day, or something else? Since the DO felt the prospective donor might later regret missing out on being involved with the new project, was the more defensible position to make sure he learned about the possibility or to honor his implication that they should leave?

In the end, the team members sought to handle an uncomfortable situation by doing what was best for both the donor and the university. They kept their lines of communication with the prospective donor open but didn't try to sell him something he said he didn't want. The outcome was that they:

- learned more about the prospective donor's company than they had known earlier.
- left the donor favorably disposed to their cause, even though he would not contribute in the way they'd originally hoped.
- had an agreement with the prospective donor on a course of action that could further their mutual interests.
- reconfirmed the donor as a friend of the university and as someone who would speak favorably of it to others.

You may be interested to know that, although many details of this case study have been changed out of respect for the person involved, the situation is based on an actual scenario the authors encountered. The sequel to the story is that, although the potential donor never did buy the naming rights to the building nor gave another gift of that magnitude, he did make a smaller, but still substantial gift to the program several years later. Acting ethically and with human decency isn't just the right thing to do; it's also a more effective way of fundraising than just focusing on immediate gain.

CONCLUDING THOUGHTS

Very few ethically questionable situations arise in academic fundraising, specifically because people make a conscious effort to violate the law or accepted practices. Problems usually arise because someone cuts corners, makes a well-intentioned effort without understanding the legal or ethical implications of that action, or is so fixated on the good resulting from a project that he or she doesn't see the complications resulting from a morally questionable decision.

Academic fundraisers who adopt a team approach are less likely to make these mistakes. Others in the group are likely to sound a note of caution before a poor decision goes too far. Knowledge of the law, AFP principles, the rights of donors, and your own instincts about what feels right or wrong are your best assets when working with ethical issues in all aspects of fundraising and community development.

For more on what world-class fundraisers need to know about ethical issues in fundraising, see the Ethics and Accountability section of the Certified Fund Raising Executive (CFRE) Examination Content Outline in Appendix III of the companion volume to this book, *World-Class Fundraising Isn't a Spectator Sport: The Team Approach to Academic Fundraising* (2016).

REFERENCES

Buller, J. L., & Reeves, D. M. (2016). *World-class fundraising isn't a spectator sport: The team approach to academic fundraising.* Lanham, MD: Rowman and Littlefield.

Grobman, G. M. (November, 2000). Fundraising ethics: Resources are only a click away. *International Journal of Nonprofit and Voluntary Sector Marketing.* 5(4), 388–390.

Mackay, H. (1988). *Swim with the sharks: Without being eaten alive.* New York, NY: William Morrow.

Rosen, M. J. (August, 2005). Doing well by doing right: A fundraiser's guide to ethical decision-making. *International Journal of Nonprofit and Voluntary Sector Marketing.* 10(3), 175–181.

RESOURCES

Briscoe, M. G. (1994). *Ethics in fundraising: Putting values into practice.* San Francisco, CA: Jossey-Bass

Elliott, D. (1995). *The ethics of asking: Dilemmas in higher education fund raising.* Baltimore, MD: Johns Hopkins University Press.

Fischer, M. (2000). *Ethical decision making in fund raising.* (6th Ed.) New York, NY: J. Wiley & Sons.

Greenfield, J. M. (2002). *Fundraising fundamentals: A guide to annual giving for professionals and volunteers.* (2nd Ed.) New York, NY: J. Wiley & Sons.

Pettey, J. G. (2013). *Nonprofit fundraising strategy: A guide to ethical decision making and regulation for nonprofit organizations.* Hoboken, NJ: Wiley.

Chapter Three

Why One Size Does Not Fit All

Many of the ethical principles of fundraising that we explored in Chapter 2 can be summarized by the familiar *Golden Rule*: Do unto others as you would have them do unto you. But world-class fundraisers know that there's a second injunction that goes beyond this one, an idea advocated by Tony Alessandra and Michael O'Connor in the title of their book *The Platinum Rule* (1998): Do unto others as *they* would have you do.

People are different, and not everyone wants to be treated in the same way. The very kind of splashy public recognition that one donor can't get enough of will mortify another donor who prefers to act behind the scenes. One of the reasons why successful fundraisers devote so much time to getting to know their donors and prospective donors well is to avoid this kind of uncomfortable mismatch between their assumptions about what a person wants and what that person really wants. Effective solicitation is highly personalized. It never assumes that one size fits all.

Much of the fundraising done at a college or university can be likened to two different types of fishing. *Net fishing* deals with quantity. As the expression "to cast a wide net" implies, it seeks to cover a large area, gathering whatever happens to fall within its net and throwing back what is undesirable, illegal, or unusable. *Spear fishing* has a much more specific target. It aims directly at one individual objective, takes sufficient time to ensure the spear is directed as precisely as possible, and only strikes when there's a high probability that the effort will meet with success. Phonathons, letter writing campaigns, and "donate now" buttons on websites are all examples of net fishing; only a small percentage of the contacts pay off, and the results are often quite small. Donor cultivation is the key to spear fishing fundraising, and it's in these efforts that successful fundraisers devote much of their time and energy.

Every donor and potential donor is different, of course, and there's no way that a single book—or even a library of books—could cover every single eventuality. But to provide a sense of how successful academic fundraisers operate by tailoring their strategies to the people they hope to recruit as donors, let's take a look at several groups that all require different approaches in fundraising, beginning with the circumstances under which someone decides to help a cause.

ISSUES OF GENDER

An experienced fundraiser would never assume that, just because a donor is a man or a woman, there are certain conclusions that can be drawn about the donor and that he or she must be treated in a particular way. Nevertheless, in the aggregate, there are a number of differences between the way in which men and women approach philanthropy that it can be useful to consider. Since the publication of Deborah Tannen's pivotal book, *You Just Don't Understand* (2013), a great deal of attention has been paid to common differences in the way in which many men and women speak, think, and perceive the world.

For example, Tannen suggests that men and women differ in how and why they speak when they're conversing with one another. At the end of a long day of work, many men want to compartmentalize. They set aside their day-time activities and refocus their attention to relaxation and leisure. As a result, they may seem to women as though they're uncommunicative about their day. When asked about what happened, they tend to say things like, "Nothing much" and leave it at that. On the other hand, women prefer to communicate the story of their day, which may appear to men to be relating a series of unrelated details. In Tannen's terms, men *report talk* (focusing on results and information) and women *rapport talk* (focusing on process and relationships).

In their book, *Women, Wealth & Giving* (2010), Margaret May Damen and Niki Nicastro McCuistion summarize interviews they held with women about their philanthropic giving. They found that women are becoming more likely to allow their names to be used in recognizing their support as leverage to encourage others to consider similar gifts. Their research also found that women are increasingly investigating charitable organizations so that they can learn how the organization is run and discover its social impact. (See Damen and McCuistion, 2010.)

Understanding these common differences can help academic fundraisers when they're communicating with potential donors. A 2010 report by the Boston Consulting Group concluded that women currently control about 27% of the world's wealth or roughly $20 trillion. Moreover, that percentage was even higher in North America, where women controlled about a third of the wealth. (www.bcg.com/documents/file56704.pdf.)

Several trends are driving this shift. One is the growth of women in the work-force. Between 1980 and 2008, the number of women in the global workforce doubled to 1.2 billion, according to the study. At the same time, more women are advancing in their careers, boosting their earning power. Women also are inher-iting more wealth. (reserve.usbank.com/pcrcp/pdfs/reservemag/Women%20 and%20Wealth.pdf.)

The result is that those involved in development must be equally effec-tive in interacting with both men and women when cultivating potential donors, volunteers, and community supporters. A 2014 study by the Bank of America found that nearly all (98.4%) people with high net worth engaged in philanthropy, with three-quarters of them also volunteering for at least one organization. Moreover, donors who volunteered contributed larger amounts than those who didn't volunteer, with approximately half of those who volun-teered saying that they did so because a nonprofit organization asked them to. (newsroom.bankofamerica.com/sites/bankofamerica.newshq.businesswire. com/files/press_kit/additional/2014_US_Trust_Study_of_High_Net_Worth_ Philanthropy_-_Executive_Summary.pdf.) "Women . . . [volunteered] at a higher rate than did men across all age groups, educational levels, and other major demographic characteristics." (www.bls.gov/news.release/volun.nr0. htm.)

Tannen's research suggests that, though there will be many individual dif-ferences, solicitations to women should often be handled differently from solicitations to men. Most men will be interested in the result: What is the project expected to accomplish, when, and at what cost? Many women, though interested in these same issues, will also want to know more about the process and the specific people who will be receiving benefits from their efforts. If men are often interested primarily in the bottom line, women who are being asked to volunteer or make a financial contribution often want to hear the story behind the project. How did it come about? Who else is involved? And how will my efforts make a difference?

Because women place a high value on the causes to which they donate their time, it is often an effective step in the cultivation phase to ask them to serve on a board or to chair an event before asking them for a donation. The type of service that men and women like to perform in their volunteer activities also tends to be different.

Collecting, preparing, distributing, or serving food (10.8 percent); fundraising (10.3 percent); and tutoring or teaching (9.3 percent) were the activities volun-teers [of both genders] performed most frequently for their main organization.

[But] men and women tended to engage in different main activities. Men who volunteered were most likely to engage in general labor (11.5 percent) or coach, referee, or supervise sports teams (9.4 percent). Female volunteers were most likely to collect, prepare, distribute, or serve food (12.1 percent); fundraise (11.6 percent); or tutor or teach (11.1 percent). (www.bls.gov/news.release/pdf/volun.pdf.)

Moreover, many financial advisors find that women make more conservative financial investments than men and are less willing to take risks in return for a potentially larger gain. (See, for example, assets.aarp.org/rgcenter/econ/women_finances_1.pdf.) As a result, they are more likely to be receptive to ideas such as charitable remainder trusts—which provide them or their beneficiaries with current income but have a corpus that reverts to the charity when they die—rather than immediate investments that may or may not retain their value.

For all these reasons, the following strategies are often useful when cultivating women as potential donors:

- Inviting them to special events in areas of their interest, including those outside of the institution itself
- Holding small-venue "work sessions" at which they'll have opportunities to network with other successful women
- Introducing them to students and professors with interests they share and providing them with extended opportunities to interact
- Including them in the planning and hosting of special educational opportunities, such as workshops on societal issues of concern, financial management, estate planning, and so on
- Inviting them to serve as mentors to students in areas of their interest
- Creating opportunities in which women can make financial contributions as a group rather than as individuals
- Assigning them to specific members of the staff with whom they can develop and maintain a long-term relationship
- Offering them leadership positions appropriate to their status and abilities and then celebrating their successes in these roles

ISSUES OF MARITAL STATUS

Issues of gender also come into play when an academic program or institution is soliciting a married couple. Although marriage is often depicted as an equal partnership, many married couples actually experience a power differential, at least in certain areas of responsibility. Moreover, it's not uncommon for each member of the couple to believe that he or she is really in charge (while claiming publicly, often in a humorous way, that it's the other person who's actually the boss). In the 2002 movie *My Big Fat Greek Wedding*, Toula Portokalos (played by Nia Vardalos) is complaining to her mother, "Ma, Dad is so stubborn. What he says goes. 'Ah, the man is the head of the house!'" Toula's mother, Maria Portokalos (portrayed by Lainie Kazan), then responds, "Let me tell you something, Toula. The man is the head, but the woman is the neck. And she can turn the head any way she wants."

World-class fundraisers are often successful because they are able to identify the dynamic at work within a married couple. It's often important to figure out whether one member of the relationship is the head (the person who outwardly appears to be making the decisions) and the other person is the neck (the person who works behind the scenes to actually control the decision that's being made). But despite how this humorous concept was introduced in the movie, those two roles are not gender specific, and they can change in different areas of decision making. A perceptive fundraiser will be aware of these dynamics when they occur and respect them throughout the cultivation process.

Frequently (although far from universally), the member of the couple who acts as the head in the area of decision making that is relevant to the proposal at hand will bring a methodical and logical approach to the discussions. This person will want to know all the details and be convinced that the business plan is sound and sustainable. The member of the couple who acts as the neck often brings a more emotional element into the discussion. He or she may feel swept away by the opportunity to do something of great significance and feel particularly moved by stories of people who can be helped by this project.

A team approach, thus, works well in this environment, since one member of the group can take the lead in discussing facts, figures, and details; whereas another member paints the picture of a compelling vision of a better future. Then, if the team engages the passion of at least one of the spouses, that person often acts as the neck, turning the cooler and more rationale head to look in the direction that he or she prefers.

In a 2009 study conducted by Fidelity Charitable Gift Fund, the authors found that most of the men who participated in their study claimed that their wives were the people who had the greatest amount of influence on their charitable decisions. (See www.fidelitycharitable.org/about-us/news/05-19-2009.shtml.) Moreover, the 2014 Bank of America Study of High Net Worth Philanthropy reported that "61 percent of respondents who are married or are living with a partner reported that they make decisions about their giving jointly with their spouse or partner. Among heterosexual married/partnered households, [only] 20 percent of women and 7 percent

of men are the sole decision-makers." (newsroom.bankofamerica.com/
sites/bankofamerica.newshq.businesswire.com/files/press_kit/additional/
2014_US_Trust_Study_of_High_Net_Worth_Philanthropy_-_Executive_
Summary.pdf.)

In many cases, husbands and wives will have overlapping but not completely congruent interests. It's important to gain a sense, therefore, whether
the project or cause the team is promoting is a matter of interest to both
spouses or primarily to one. As the Bank of America study mentioned earlier, the ability to make clear, major financial contributions usually requires
extensive discussion and agreement between the spouses. Even when the
couples don't feel "required" to get approval from one another for these
contributions, most of them at least discuss large expenditures before
proceeding.

As a result, if the institution is dealing with one member of a couple in the
hope of obtaining a large, transformative gift, it's sound practice to bring the
spouse into the discussion at some point before the ask occurs. In this way,
preplanning and coordination of the proposal with both members of the couple will help the process run more smoothly. In fact, when this involvement
of the husband and wife is handled effectively, the ask itself often proves to
be only a formality; the couple already has expressed its consensus that it
will help.

As marriage equality becomes increasingly common, the couples with
whom academic fundraisers interact will no longer be exclusively heterosexual. Same-sex couples bring many of the same dynamics with them that
are found in any marriage: There may be a pretense of equality when actual
power differentials exist; one member may be more overt as a decision maker,
whereas the other tends to act behind the scenes; and major gifts will often
require substantial discussion and consensus.

Since successful fundraisers realize that these roles aren't gender specific
in heterosexual couples, they bring no preconceived notions about these roles
to same-sex couples either. Instead, they use their understanding of human
nature and sensitivity to individual differences as resources for bringing all
couples the types of information and insights they need in order to make the
most appropriate philanthropic decisions for their interests and plans.

ISSUES OF GENERATION

A great deal of discussion—some of it based on serious research but much
of it fanciful—has been devoted to the personalities and characteristics of
different generations. Put rather simplistically, much of this discussion boils
down to the following:

- *The Greatest Generation* (born 1900–1945) was tested by the twin crucibles of the Great Depression and World War II. This generation is practical, conformist, hardworking, and patriotic.
- *Baby Boomers* (born 1946–1964) were the center of attention due to their numbers throughout the 1950s and 1960s. They were influenced by hippies and the antiwar movement and, thus, tend to challenge authority, be devoted to equal rights for all, cling to their youth even as they age, and want to distance themselves from their parents.
- *Generation X* (born 1965–1980) were shaped by events such as the Watergate scandal and the end of the Cold War. They are skeptical to the point of cynicism, more practical than their parents, self-reliant, and highly educated.
- *Millennials* or *Generation Y* (born 1981 and after) are the children of Baby Boomers or Generation X parents and often had every available moment of their young lives scheduled with activities, sports, and clubs. They are quite attached to their parents, confident they they'll succeed (and thus often unprepared for failure), technically proficient, devoted to fun, and consumer oriented.

Like our discussions of gender and marital status, such broad stereotypes only go so far. We all know individuals who are completely different from the way in which their generations are commonly described, just as we all know couples who don't seem to fit any of the patterns we discussed earlier and people who deviate completely from traditional gender roles.

Nevertheless, even if we don't hold firmly to the concept that different generations have their own distinct, collective personalities and values, it's important for academic fundraisers to be aware that young successful entrepreneurs sometimes do think about philanthropy differently from their more senior counterparts who grew up within a corporate culture.

Moreover, that difference is a bit more substantive than a preference for handwritten thank you notes or concise text messages. As an indication of how important it can be to be responsive to the specific worldview of different generations, the authors present the following case study, fictionalized in some of its details but based on one of their actual experiences.

CLOSING A DEAL WITH A HANDSHAKE

Most business deals today are considered completed only when the ink is dry and the lawyers have reviewed every possible detail. Even then, there might be modifications later as one party or another claims that the situation has changed and the original agreement is no longer adequate. But not every prospective donor came of age in such a litigious business environment. There was once a time when a handshake was all that people needed to seal a deal, and some members of the community still live by these principles.

The university was actively seeking donors who were interested in acquiring naming rights for a program it had created in 1999. One of the potential donors approached by the office of institutional advancement was someone we'll call Gene Greatest, a member of the Greatest Generation who had never earlier made a gift to the university, even though he had been generous in supporting other educational institutions, as well as local hospitals, museums, and zoos.

The development officer (DO) had had Mr. Greatest on her radar screen for some time and had been trying to interest him in the university. They spoke on the phone periodically for nearly a year, although the calls were often rather brief. Mr. Greatest seemed to be a man of few words and even his voicemail messages contained nothing more than a terse request for a call back or a quick bit of follow-up information. During one particular phone call, however, he began to drift into more personal areas. He mentioned that his wife passed away just a year earlier and that she had been the person who handled the planning of their social life. As a result, he didn't go out much anymore, not because he didn't like parties and receptions, but because he'd never really had to plan one earlier.

The DO suggested that she'd be happy to organize an event of this kind. She booked a private room at a local restaurant and personally selected about forty guests who would include a number of local dignitaries as well as representatives of the university. That night, a specially selected group—the president of the university, the administrator in charge of the new program, several faculty members and students carefully chosen for their social skills, and the DO herself—would sit with Mr. Greatest at the head table.

The night arrived, and everything was working out perfectly. The weather was mild and clear, and so the city sparkled through the large windows all around the dining room. The tables were tastefully set. Gift bags, filled with chocolates and promotional items about the program, were placed discreetly by each seat. Guests began to arrive. Everyone took his or her assigned seat. Music played softly in the background. There was only one thing wrong: Mr. Greatest was nowhere to be found.

The DO excused herself and repeatedly tried to call the guest of honor. He didn't answer his phone, and even his voicemail didn't appear to be working. Eventually, there was a decision to start the dinner anyway in the hope that Mr. Greatest would join them later. But he never showed up, and there was no message to explain his absence. The DO was embarrassed by this outcome and decided that Mr. Greatest must just be someone they couldn't count on.

"People are like that sometimes," she thought. "They let you down, and their word doesn't mean a thing. I guess I'd better chalk this one up to experience."

The next day, the DO tried to call Mr. Greatest again, assuming that one last call might bring closure to the whole, unpleasant situation. This time, however, instead of ringing endlessly, the line was busy. The DO tried calling off and on for more than four hours, and each time she reached a busy signal. "He must be putting together some kind of business deal," she thought, her annoyance growing. "Either that or stringing along some other charity."

Finally, late in the afternoon, she called again, and this time the house-keeper answered. It immediately became clear why the previous evening had gone as it did: Mr. Greatest had suffered a serious fall while getting ready for the event. He had been taken to the emergency room and then admitted to the hospital. As soon as the housekeeper had arrived that morning, Mr. Greatest had called her and told her to get in touch with the university to offer his deepest and most sincere apologies. He would have called himself but he didn't have any of the phone numbers he needed with him in the hospital. That's why the telephone at the house had been busy so long that day: The housekeeper had been trying to track down the DO to explain the situation. But without a name or any other information to go on, she was never able to get through to the right person.

The DO was ashamed that she had thought so poorly of Mr. Greatest when he didn't show up at the party. She called the administrator in charge of the new program, and together they went to the hospital to visit their long-overdue guest. When they got to his room, Mr. Greatest looked quite frail, even older than the DO had assumed. They waited until he woke up and, almost as soon as he opened his eyes and discovered who they were, he began to apologize again for missing what he was sure had been a wonderful party.

They assured him that they fully understood the situation and were only concerned about his fall. Mr. Greatest downplayed his health challenges and said that the only thing he felt bad about was giving them his word he'd be at the dinner but then not being able to keep his promise. He said he was touched that they would make a special trip to check on him and that he'd love to meet with them again in the near future. The administrator and DO didn't not want to tax his strength, so they left quickly, agreeing to visit him at his home sometime soon.

Thus began what the DO began to call her "Fridays with Gene," after Mitch Albom's popular book *Tuesdays with Morrie* (1997). At the end of each week, they'd get together for a few hours, sometimes sharing lunch at a restaurant, at other times just talking at Mr. Greatest's home. Over the course of several months, he began to open up more and more. He had very strong political views, but he never seemed to mind when the DO took issue with something he said.

Eventually, their meetings reached the point where they felt comfortable just sitting with one another, even if there were long silences. It was the most unusual cultivation phase the DO had ever known. Other members of the development staff were still involved, but they were working behind the scenes. This particular donor seemed to prefer casual meetings with the DO to anything more formal, and the team decided it was best to respect this preference.

One day, out of the blue, Mr. Greatest asked the DO whether she could help him with one of the other philanthropic efforts he'd been working on. Once again, she was disappointed that he never said anything about helping the university, but she decided to do what she could to assist him, hoping it might still lead to his support of the (now no longer new) academic program. She contributed a great deal of research time to get Mr. Greatest the most current and accurate information she could, and their weekly meetings became a mixture of conversation and working sessions.

After several more months of work, he mentioned that perhaps the project to help his other philanthropic interest could somehow serve the university too. Since there didn't appear to be any obvious connection between the two projects, the DO had to work feverishly behind the scenes to see whether there was some way in which the university could legally provide offices for the other charity or do anything at all that might bring the two causes together.

The next Friday, during the DO's regular meeting with Mr. Greatest, she mentioned an idea the team had developed of constructing a new building that could provide space for both the new academic program and the other charity he was interested in. The building could be named after Mr. Greatest or anyone he wished and would require an accompanying endowment to ensure that maintenance and program support remained adequately funded for the future.

They were sitting at Mr. Greatest's dining room table at the time, and his attention seemed distracted by the various building concepts and drawings the DO had brought along to the meeting. "And how much would all of that cost me?" Mr. Greatest asked, without looking up. "Twenty-five million dollars," the DO said, trying to keep the quiver out of her voice.

Without saying a word, Mr. Greatest then extended his hand for the DO to shake. When he looked up, she must have still had a puzzled look on her face. "That means," he explained, "that we are in agreement." There was a brief pause. He must have thought that even that statement wasn't clear enough. "In other words, we have a deal. Let's do something wonderful."

Even though his hands had been shaking with age, the firmness of his grip left no doubt as to his sincerity. Tears welled up in the DO's eyes and, as she looked at Mr. Greatest, she could see his eyes were moist as well.

Back at the university, the vice president for development was incredulous. "Oral agreements don't mean a thing. We need to get a contract. Put him in touch with our lawyers." But the DO knew that this was exactly the wrong approach. If anything could derail the project at this point, it would be a sudden transition from a conversational relationship to a legalistic one. The proper paperwork would, of course, have to come. But that could be handled between Mr. Greatest's legal advisors and the university's office of legal affairs.

An oral commitment for a $25 million gift may have been unusual, but it was generationally appropriate. In Mr. Greatest's long life, he had built a successful business on more verbal deals than written contracts. Ever since she had seen the look on his face in the hospital when he said, "But I gave you my word," the DO knew he was a person whose word was his bond and who expected others to live up to the same principles.

Mr. Greatest believed in relationships more than contracts, and the extended cultivation process was the only way the gift could be obtained. As expected, the legal teams worked out the terms of the gift agreement, and Mr. Greatest was invited to the president's office to sign the official document, the only time he met other members of the university's administrative staff.

Even after the funds had been transferred, the DO and Mr. Greatest continued their weekly meetings. But he never again mentioned philanthropy or expressed any interest in meeting with anyone from the university other than the DO. Three years later, Mr. Greatest died peacefully in his sleep. The program he funded and the building he named now continue his memory.

ISSUES OF NET WORTH

Working with a donor such as Gene Greatest required a tailored approach due to the expectations he had as a member of his generation. But there were also distinctive aspects to this process because of the donor's wealth and background. In his short story "The Snows of Kilimanjaro," Ernest Hemingway put into the mouth of one of his characters an exchange he sometimes claimed he himself had had with F. Scott Fitzgerald. "He remembered poor Julian and his romantic awe of [the wealthy] and how he had started a story once that began, 'the very rich are different from you and me.' And how someone had said to Julian, Yes, they have more money." (Hemingway, 1977, 76–77.) In fact, Fitzgerald's statement was far more nuanced than Hemingway implies and appears in the third paragraph of his own short story "The Rich Boy."

> Let me tell you about the very rich. They are different from you and me. They possess and enjoy early, and it does something to them, makes them soft, where we are hard, cynical where we are trustful, in a way that, unless you were born rich, it is very difficult to understand. They think, deep in their hearts, that they

are better than we are because we had to discover the compensations and refuges of life for ourselves. Even when they enter deep into our world or sink below us, they still think that they are better than we are. They are different. (Fitzgerald, 1926, 1–2)

Whether you agree with Hemingway or Fitzgerald, one thing is clear: When you're dealing with very wealthy potential donors, you need to tailor your style and strategy so as to increase the likelihood of a successful outcome. In his book, *Wealth in Families* (2012), Charles W. Collier, a former senior philanthropic adviser at Harvard University, builds on the work of James E. Hughes, Jr. (2004) about the four main types of family capital and how they affect the outlook of the very wealthy.

The first type of family capital is the one that most people think of immediately: *financial wealth*. But the approach that a family takes to its financial assets can vary widely. Some families rarely talk about levels of wealth until a bequest is revealed. Some parents teach their children at an early age how to earn, save, and give back to society. Others invite their young adult children into the decision-making process of researching social programs and discussing why they would suggest supporting particular organizations and not others. These discussions sometimes grow into roles of increasing importance as children are given added responsibilities in the structure and governance of a family foundation or a nonprofit organization to which the family has close associations.

But wealth is not the only type of capital that's important in families that have a high net worth. Three other resources that are equally important but less well recognized by the general public are *human capital, intellectual capital*, and *social capital*.

> Human capital refers to who individual family members are, and what they are called to do; intellectual capital refers to how family members learn and govern themselves; social capital denotes how family members engage with society at large; and financial capital stands for the property of the family. (Collier, 2012, 8)

When wealthy people use the expression "life is rich," they're often referring to assets other than financial wealth, such as close family ties, good friendships with interesting people, and close social engagement.

Ginie Sayles, who has made a career out of demystifying the practices and attitudes of the very wealthy, goes even further than Collier by saying that there are fourteen layers of class.

1. Financial wealth or affluence
2. Distinguished lineage
3. Memberships in exclusive clubs and organizations

4. Education at a prestigious college or university, an advanced degree from any accredited university, or both
5. Patronage and appreciation of the arts
6. Familiarity with how to socialize with others of high net worth and comfort in doing so
7. Knowledge of and involvement in political causes
8. Ease in traveling among foreign cultures
9. Knowledge of and participation in sports
10. Adherence to a set of principles that values people rather than possessions, individual differences, or other external factors
11. Etiquette (behaving properly in each situation) and manners (acting in such a way as to put others at ease)
12. Interesting hobbies
13. Philanthropy
14. Achievements

(Sayles, 2008)

Families with high net worth frequently engage in philanthropic activities because they feel a social obligation—the modern equivalent of the more traditional *noblesse oblige*—or because they care about an issue so deeply that they want to have a positive impact on the future. The key is for academic fundraisers to understand what a wealthy family's perspective of the world happens to be and what values resonate with that family so strongly that it will be moved to contribute to that cause.

At most colleges and universities, it will largely be the responsibility of the DO to discover what he or she can about these motivations and share this information with the others. The DO will conduct research by learning where the family has made its previous philanthropic commitments, in what amounts those contributions were made, and which family member took the lead in promoting that cause.

Some institutions have large research offices that assist the development staff with uncovering this background information. Others will expect the DO to discover this information independently. In either case, it will be important for the person who conducts this research to understand the sources of public information that are available and how to interpret them.

The social circles in which the very wealthy participate often have codes that differ from those of other groups. For example, people who meet with prospective donors may wish to have in their possession both business cards (which give their professional title, affiliation, and contact information) and social cards (which list only their name and personal contact information). When meeting someone for the first time at a social gathering, wealthy people may consider it rude to be handed their new acquaintance's business card rather than a social card since it implies that the person views the new relationship as a potential source of financial gain.

There are unstated rules about what to wear at various events, and someone dressing either too formally or informally could be considered unrefined. Nevertheless, on certain other occasions, a wealthy prospective donor may expect certain forms of dress within his or her own circle—such as men wearing shoes without socks at informal events in warm weather—that would be considered out of place for an employee of a university who is known to be "on the clock."

Other practices such as knowing when to applaud at a concert or recital, where to rest a knife and fork to indicate that one is finished with that course of a meal, and how to address a member of the nobility can sometimes be learned from books but are more often simply acquired through experience. They're among the ways in which people with inherited wealth may distinguish whether a newcomer is "one of us."

In addition to outlining the different layers of class, Ginie Sayles distinguishes eight different kinds of social events that the very wealthy often host and attend.

1. Coffees (morning) and teas (afternoon): small, formal social gatherings
2. Weekend brunches: a combination of a coffee and a cocktail party
3. Cocktail parties: early evening events at which guests are expected to stand and mingle
4. Weekend country getaways: somewhat structured events for a small group of houseguests at a country house or beach house
5. Black tie events (such as formal dinners and certain holiday events): formal events that require a tuxedo or dinner jacket for men and gowns appropriate to the season for women
6. White tie events: balls and extremely formal events that require tail coats for men and full-length ball gowns from women
7. Formal dinners in estates and mansions: very traditional, highly structured dinners that are preceded by cocktails and hors d'oeuvres accompanied by background music, composed of multiple courses, served by a professional staff, and usually scheduled not to begin until 9:00 or 10:00 pm
8. After-theater meals: less formal dinners with a small group of friends after a play, concert, or other type of live performance.

(Sayles, 2013)

Each of these events has its own dress code, expected forms of behavior, expectations for hostess gifts, and timing (i.e., when to arrive and when to leave). Successful academic fundraisers are those who become familiar with all these variations and are capable of engaging in light conversation with anyone. If you're a person for whom it is difficult to know what to say when meeting strangers, some helpful resources include Debra Fine's *The Fine Art of Small Talk* (2005), Mary Lou Walker and Matthew Calkins' *Speak Easy* (2010), and Leil Lowndes' *How to Instantly Connect with Anyone* (2009).

INTERACTING WITH PARENTS

As everyone who works in higher education can attest, the current generation of college students has parents who tend to remain highly involved in every aspect of their children's education. It's not uncommon for parents of students to call the dean, provost, or even president to discuss a problem with a course. Occasionally, even the parent of a graduate student will attempt to intervene in an academic issue affecting his or her child.

Large numbers of parents view the Family Educational Rights and Privacy Act (FERPA: U.S. Code1232g; 34 CFR Part 99) not as legislation that guarantees their children's rights to the privacy of their educational records, but as an undesirable impediment to their own involvement in their children's education. They wonder why colleges and universities don't make it easier for students to waive their FERPA rights or perhaps even instruct them to do so. They want their children to be completely safe and yet to have complete freedom. They expect that they'll be informed if their son or daughter fails to come to class, receives an unsatisfactory grade, or changes his or her major. All this energy and concern can be wonderful if it's directed to some productive purpose rather than hindering the students' ability to solve their own problems and receive the quality of education they deserve.

One way for a college or university to address this challenge is to create a formal parents' council. Parents' councils can be created on behalf of an entire institution, or they may be sponsored by specific colleges or departments. Serving on a parents' council channels the energy and desire to help (which many parents have) toward projects that institutions and their individual units actually need.

In order to achieve this goal, however, it is helpful to develop a charter or a set of bylaws for the group that clearly specifies what the council does and does not do. If you provide no restrictions of the responsibilities of a parents' council, it will soon try to advise you on matters such as which new programs you should develop, how much money you should raise and for what purpose, which faculty members you should promote or terminate, and how budgetary priorities should be set.

One proviso to keep in mind, however, is that calling any group an *advisory* council encourages its members to offer you advice—even in areas for which you do not want to be advised and areas about which the members know very little. For this reason, most institutions will want to steer clear of names such as Parents Advisory Council and to set out very specific guidelines for the group's operating procedures. The most desirable situation is to develop a charter for the group that outlines particular areas of concern for the council—such as recruitment of new students, fundraising, and community relations—while stating that all other matters remain outside the purview of the council.

Members of a parents' council can be wonderful representatives at college fairs, particularly at institutions where the admissions staff finds it difficult to attend all the programs that are available throughout the region. Parents can:

- speak directly to parents of prospective students and discuss the benefits that an institution or its curriculum had for their own children.
- host receptions for prospective students or, even better, for students in their area who have been admitted but who have not yet agreed to attend the school.
- recommend specific students to the institution, help admitted students move in on opening day, and attend open house events.
- improve retention by serving as mentors for students who have issues they don't want to discuss with their own parents or by providing introductions to professionals who work in fields where students hope to find internships or employment.

For academic fundraisers, however, the most important role of a parents' council comes in development work. Because they have direct buy into the mission of the institution, members of a parents' council are more likely to contribute to a school's annual fund themselves and to encourage others to do so. Rather than a letter from a dean or president asking parents to contribute to a school's annual fund, a letter from another parent inviting the reader to "join me in giving" can provide a powerful appeal.

At a meeting with a prospective donor, a parent can provide a perspective that an employee of the institution doesn't have. A parent's voice is often less suspect than a statement made by a paid employee because they receive no direct benefit from advocating on behalf of the institution. Parents can open doors with leaders in their own fields and areas, providing contacts that the development office might not otherwise have.

When staffing phonathons or planning galas, members of a parents' council supply a ready source of enthusiastic labor and often feel grateful even for being asked to help. They can host fundraising events in their homes, invite prospective donors to lunch with the dean or the president, and lead fundraising initiatives, particularly those that have a direct impact on the experience of their children.

As might be expected, parents tend to be more greatly involved in fundraising activities that can be tied in some way to the benefit of current students than those that will largely serve later generations. A building that won't be constructed for a decade probably won't garner the same level of support as renovations to the student union that could be completed this year. Other effective strategies for engaging parents in fundraising activities involve campaigns that can be linked in some way to the parent's own children. For example, parents are often attracted to campaigns built around a student's class year. So, for students who are expected to graduate in the year 2020, it's useful to build giving levels around that number: $20.20, $202.00, $2,020, and so on.

Similarly, parents of current students are often the most active in promoting events that they feel will interest their children, their children's friends, and their own associates in the community. When that occurs, parents can provide word-of-mouth advertising for lecture series, travel programs, and other special events that are hosted by an institution.

For first-time parents of college students, members of a parents' council can offer a sympathetic ear for concerns and a supportive voice when advice is necessary. They can provide volunteer labor for printed or electronic newsletters, mass mailings, and e-mail blasts. They can serve as greeters at campus events, reinforcing the campus' reputation as a friendly and welcoming place, distribute fliers, and contact their local media when student achievements need to be highlighted. They can help smooth troubled town/gown relations, since they effectively have a foot in each of these "camps."

If you're considering the establishment or revitalization of a parents' council as part of your development efforts, two useful places to begin are the Association of Higher Education Parent/Family Program Professionals, which holds national and regional conferences and provides links to many electronic resources on its website (www.aheppp.org), and College Parents of America, which is an organization for parents of current and future college students that can help you stay in touch with issues of concern to this important group of stakeholders (www.collegeparents.org).

One other approach that academic fundraisers may find effective is to establish a parents' council that automatically includes the parents of all currently enrolled students, whereas an executive board of this council— consisting of perhaps ten to twenty parents who have demonstrated a strong interest in becoming more active—sets the agendas for meetings, runs those meetings, and plans yearly events for the larger group.

As long as the group's mission and areas of concern are carefully focused, the creation of a parents' council can be an excellent approach to the challenge presented by parents who have a great desire to become involved in their children's education but relatively little knowledge of the most effective way to achieve this goal.

CASE STUDY

Ritzy Glamour is a wealthy toothpick heiress who lives with her family on an estate in the exclusive community of Palm Hampton. The Glamour fortune was made when Ritzy's grandfather invented the double-ended toothpick, thus immediately increasing the efficiency of his company's product by 100%. Ritzy further increased her fortune when she became the fifth wife of Supercilious P. Glamour, the famous magnet magnate. The entire Glamour family has supported the university for quite some time, and the vice president of development thinks that the time may be near when a sizable donation would be possible, if the institution cultivates the family properly.

The university has recently hired a new provost, Dr. Naïve N. Kluliss, and so the vice president of development is delighted when Ritzy's social secretary calls to inquire about the possibility of Dr. Kluliss and a few other university representatives attending a morning coffee the next Thursday, which would be followed by a small luncheon. The secretary says that Ritzy is hoping to introduce the university leadership to two of her most important groups of friends: a few members of her tennis club, who would join them for the coffee, and the executive committee of the Sibelius Society of Palm Hampton who would attend the luncheon. Details are quickly arranged, and the vice president discusses the importance of this event with the new provost.

On the day of the event, Dr. Kluliss travels separately in her own car because she has another meeting near Palm Hampton scheduled for that afternoon. The invitation for the coffee was for 9:00 am, so the provost, not wanting to make a bad impression by arriving late, knocks on the door of Glamour Cottage promptly at 8:40 am. While waiting for the hostess and other guests to arrive, she learns from the staff what she can about Ritzy and Supercilious Glamour, so that she'll have plenty to talk about during the coffee and luncheon.

Everyone has been saying that the Glamours are very traditional and "old money," so Dr. Kluliss was sure to have her best black pantsuit freshly laundered and pressed to make sure that her own elegance would reflect that of her environment.

As soon as her hostess came downstairs, the provost told her how lovely the house was and how fortunate she must feel living in such an expensive area as Palm Hampton. She was careful, though, not to monopolize too much of Ritzy's time, and so she ended their conversation as soon as the first guest arrived and went up to introduce herself.

As each person arrived for the coffee, Dr. Kluliss handed the person she was talking to her business card, told that person that she'd be happy to continue this discussion at another time, and went up to introduce herself to the next new arrival. When the coffee was winding down, Dr. Kluliss thanked all the guests for coming and told them what an honor it had been to meet them.

Pleased with how well things were going, Dr. Kluliss continued to speak to each guest as the members of the Sibelius Society of Palm Hampton began arriving to the luncheon. When a staff member opened the doors to the sun porch for the luncheon, Dr. Kluliss made sure that Ritzy Glamour entered first, saw that she was sitting at the head of the table, and took the seat immediately to Ritzy's left so that they'd have a chance to talk further over the meal.

She had plenty of questions for her hostess about the toothpick and magnet industries, how many rooms the estate had, and which programs at the university the Glamours most wanted to fund. When she noticed that a nearby side table had a photograph of Mr. Glamour with several adult children, Dr. Kluliss complimented Ritzy by saying that she was sure the children got their good looks from their mother. She was impressed by Ritzy's modesty when she merely smiled politely and didn't respond.

When the meal was over, she carefully laid her knife and fork on her napkin to avoid soiling the tablecloth, thanked her hostess for the invitation, mentioned that she had another appointment in town, and took her leave of the guests. About half an hour later, Ritzy told everyone at the table how pleased she was that so many members of the Sibelius Society's distinguished board could attend the day's luncheon, thanked them for coming, and hoped they'd all enjoyed themselves.

One by one, the guests took their leave of Ritzy, thanking her for such a wonderful event. When the DO reached her hostess to thank her, Ritzy said, "Yes, I'd love to have you and perhaps your president come join me sometime for a tea. But I believe not your new provost. I'm sure you understand."

The DO said, "Of course. And a tea with the president sounds lovely. If your social secretary will call me, we'll make some time available. Thank you again for such a wonderful coffee and luncheon." As the team drove back toward campus, the DO kept asking herself, "What in the world did Dr. Kluliss do?"

QUESTIONS

1. What mistakes did Dr. Kluliss make that seem to have alienated Ritzy Glamour?
2. How should the other members of the university administration now respond so as to salvage this situation?

POSSIBLE STRATEGIES

The following are some of the gaffes D. Kluliss made that could have alienated Ritzy Glamour.

- An arrival at 8:40 am is far too early for a coffee that begins at 9:00 am. The optimal time to arrive at a formal 9:00 am event at someone's home is 9:05 am, not too early so that the guest seems overly eager or punctilious, not so late as to seem indifferent to the host or hostess' schedule.
- It's poor form to make inquiries to the staff about the host or hostess. They're encouraged to be discreet, so these questions put them in an awkward position. At large homes or estates, guests are expected to be served by the staff, and hence, guests should not strike up prolonged conversations with them.
- For a very traditional host or hostess, black clothing would seem far too formal for a morning event.
- For a very traditional host or hostess, any type of pantsuit may well seem excessively informal or out of place.
- It was acceptable for Dr. Kluliss to mention that the Glamours have a lovely home, but her reference to Palm Hampton as an expensive area to live would seem inappropriate and crassly commercial.
- Although it is desirable to mingle with all the guests at a coffee, the way in which Dr. Kluliss broke off each conversation as soon as the next person entered the room would have seemed abrupt, even rude.
- Handing each person a business card (rather than a social card) at an event such as a morning coffee would probably be regarded as tacky at best.
- It wasn't Dr. Kluliss' place to thank the guests for coming to the coffee. By doing so, she usurped the role of her hostess.
- Since the guests of the Sibelius Society were probably of mixed gender (and almost certainly planned to be so by Ritzy or her social secretary), a very traditional hostess would want her guests to sit with alternating men and women.
- By sitting at Ritzy's left, Dr. Kluliss complicated the situation even further, since, at traditional events, the man is expected to assist the woman to his right with her chair and to engage her regularly in light conversation.
- Dr. Kluliss' conversation was anything but light. By talking about the toothpick and magnet industries, she focused the topic on business. By bluntly asking about a possible gift to the university, she turned a subtle cultivation visit into a solicitation visit. She also returned to the issue of how large the Glamours' home was, giving the entire conversation an unnecessarily commercial cast.

- Since Supercilious Glamour had had a number of previous marriages, it was presumptive of Dr. Kluliss to assume that the children in the photograph were Ritzy's, particularly since she wasn't in the picture. If, indeed, the children had a different mother, Dr. Kluliss' remark that the children must have received their good looks from their mother was a faux pas at best. If Ritzy had thought the remark was intentional, it could even have been taken as an insult.
- It's inappropriate to put a soiled knife and fork on top of the napkin on the table. When a guest is finished eating, the knife and fork should be placed on the plate alongside one another, with the tines of the fork up and the serrated edge of the knife facing the fork, with handles at the lower right of the plate and tops aimed toward the upper left (like a clock with its hands at 4:20).
- Even though one may occasionally be forgiven for leaving an event early, Dr. Kluliss did so very abruptly and probably left behind the impression that she had to be somewhere that she regarded as more important. If she absolutely had to leave, that should have been made clear to the social secretary well before the event, and Dr. Kluliss should have departed more gracefully.

In order to handle the situation more properly in the future, there are two courses of action that need to be taken. First, Dr. Kluliss needs to engage in some training in formal etiquette. If she's going to continue to remain involved in the institution's fundraising efforts, she'll need to learn how to dress, act, and speak in a variety of social situations. It's clear from the case study that she has had very little preparation in this area.

One tactful way in which this training might be given is for the president to mention at a senior staff meeting, "Every now and then, I find myself in social situations where I can't remember what all the expectations are. I think it'd be a good idea for all of us to work with an etiquette consultant that I'll be bringing in. It shouldn't take long and, even if you already know all this stuff—and I'm sure most of you do—a refresher every now and then is a useful thing. I know I could benefit from this kind of training."

That course of action deals in a long-term manner with Dr. Kluliss' weaknesses. But a second strategy ought to be considered as a way of making sure that the institution's relationship with Glitzy Glamour remains on track. At least in the short term, the prospective donor's wishes should be honored, and meetings should be held without Dr. Kluliss. Since Ritzy Glamour appears to have the capacity to make a very large gift, it may even be desirable to have the president step in, charm the Glamours, and try to put the awkward incident behind them.

It will depend on the personalities of the donors, of course, but it's often a wise practice not to apologize for the mishandled meeting—reminding donors of an incident they would probably rather forget is often counterproductive— and simply to proceed with greater sensitivity, tact, and refinement. Once Dr. Kluliss has been properly prepared in the expectations of prospective donors such as the Glamours, she can be gradually reintroduced to the process if her presence is deemed essential to the project.

Academic fundraisers will sometimes encounter situations where, for whatever reason, a donor or prospective donor prefers not to deal with them. Although it will sometimes be due to something a member said or did, as in this case study, more frequently people simply find that they have better rapport with certain representatives of the institution than others. When that occurs, a good team player doesn't take it personally. After all, the goal is the good of the institution, not personal pride or feelings. It's only when a donor specifically alludes to inappropriate behavior on the part of one particular person, as Ritzy Glamour did, or multiple donors request not to interact with a specific individual that the question arises as to whether that person should be involved in fundraising efforts at all.

CONCLUDING THOUGHTS

By recognizing that donors often have different expectations depending on their gender, family status, age, wealth, and other factors, world-class academic fundraisers don't assume that a married woman who's a wealthy baby boomer will automatically respond to one type of cultivation whereas a Generation X bachelor from a humble background will automatically respond to another. In fact, the point of this chapter is precisely the opposite.

Each donor or potential donor is a unique individual who will have his or her own view of the world, preferences for interacting with the institution, and expectations for the people with whom he or she interacts. By being aware that these factors sometimes vary by gender, generation, social status, and other issues, academic fundraisers will be able to develop sensitivity to the individual personality of each constituent with whom they work.

REFERENCES

Albom, M. (1997). *Tuesdays with Morrie: An old man, a young man, and life's great-est lesson.* New York, NY: Doubleday.

Alessandra, A. J., & O'Connor, M. J. (1998). *The platinum rule: Discover the four basic business personalities—and how they can lead you to success.* New York, NY: Warner.

Collier, C. W. (2012). *Wealth in families.* Cambridge, MA: Harvard University Press.

Damen, M. M., & and McCuistion, N. N. (2010). *Women, wealth & giving.* Hoboken, NJ: Wiley.

Fine, D. (2005). *The fine art of small talk: How to start a conversation, keep it going, build networking skills, and leave a positive impression.* New York, NY: Hyperion.

Fitzgerald, F. S. (1926). *All the sad young men.* New York, NY: Charles Scribner's Sons.

Gottlieb, H. (2008). *The Pollyanna principles: Reinventing "nonprofit organizations" to create the future of our world.* Tucson, AZ: Renaissance.

Hemingway, E. (1977). *The first forty-nine stories.* Franklin Center, PA: Franklin Library.

Hughes, J. E. (2004). *Family wealth: Keeping it in the family: How family members and their advisers preserve human, intellectual, and financial assets for generations.* New York, NY: Bloomberg Press.

Lowndes, L. (2009). *How to instantly connect with anyone.* New York, NY: McGraw-Hill.

Sayles, G. (2013). *Entertaining the rich (audiorecording).* Dallas, TX: Ginie Sayles Enterprises.

Sayles, G. (2008). *The 14 layers of class (audiorecording).* Dallas, TX: Ginie Sayles Enterprises.

Tannen, D. (2013). *You just don't understand: Women and men in conversation.* New York, NY: Harper.

Walker, M. L., & Calkins, M. (2010). *Speak easy: Mary Lou's rules for engaging conversation.* Lafayette, CA: Cupola Press.

RESOURCES

Clift, E. (2005). *Women, philanthropy, and social change: Visions for a just society.* Hanover, NH: University Press of New England.

Fussell, P. (1984). *Class: A guide through the American status system.* New York, NY: Ballantine Books.

Shaw, H. (2013). *Sticking points: How to get 4 generations working together in the 12 places they come apart.* Carol Stream, IL: Tyndale House.

Shaw-Hardy, S. C., Beaudoin-Schwartz, B., & Taylor, M. A. (2010). *Women and philanthropy: Boldly shaping a better world.* San Francisco, CA: Jossey-Bass.

Smith, K. C. (2007). *The top 10 distinctions between millionaires and the middle class.* New York, NY: Ballantine.

Zemke, R., Raines, C., & Filipczak, B. (2003). *Generations at work: Managing the clash of veterans, boomers, xers, and nexters in your workplace.* New York, NY: AMACOM.

Chapter Four

The SPORT of Giving and the ACID Test

Once academic fundraisers have become thoroughly familiar with essential fundraising principles, the ethical standards that will guide their activities, and how to tailor their approaches toward individual donors, it's time for them to begin going for the gold by cultivating actual donors and soliciting actual gifts. In order to be successful in these efforts, it's helpful to become acquainted with a concept that the authors call *the SPORT of giving*.

THE SPORT OF GIVING

As we saw in Chapter 3, not all donors are alike. Just because a certain strategy has worked earlier when cultivating and soliciting a donor, there's no guarantee that this same strategy will be equally effective with someone whose background, needs, and interests are completely different from that donor. Some people will be attracted to philanthropy because of the tax advantages a gift will bring, others will be interested in the prestige that results from the gift, and still others will be attracted by the benefits and perks that an organization provides its donors.

In addition, in her book *The Pollyanna Principles* (2009), Hildy Gottlieb describes the importance of knowing whether a prospective donor is interested in solving a specific problem or in contributing toward a more general vision of a better world. (See Gottlieb, 2009, 54.) The difference is that problem-solving donations are best tied to individual projects in which results, or at least tangible progress, can be measured rather quickly.

Vision-based donations tend to occur when fundraisers focus on long-range goals, some of which are idealistic and possibly even unattainable. For example, a problem-solving donor is likely to contribute to a program that rehabilitates drug users, whereas a vision-based donor would be more interested in educational programs that discourage drug use before it even starts.

Other types of giving and the circumstances under which they occur can be more easily remembered if we refer to them by the acronym *SPORT*.

- *S*pot-or "on-the-spot" giving occurs when a person gives spontaneously to a cause largely because an opportunity arises. A few examples of spot giving include purchasing a box of Girl Scout cookies at a table set up in front of a grocery store, dropping some coins into the guitar case of a street performer, or handing a few small bills to a homeless person who is soliciting donations on a street corner.

  In higher education, spot giving might occur when current students make cold calls to members of the community or when a program has a booth at a home football game. Most donors who engage in spot giving haven't devoted a great deal of forethought to the contribution they make. They simply decide to offer a gift (which is usually quite small) because an opportunity happens to arise.
- *P*lanned giving is the exact opposite of spot giving. As a technical term in fundraising, the expression *planned giving* refers to larger gifts that someone makes as a bequest and only fulfills after his or her death.

  More generally, however, the type of giving that we have in mind involves any large gift of sufficient complexity that requires substantial preparation, often in the form of legal counsel, in order for it to be prepared, executed, and received. For this reason, all types of trusts may be considered planned giving, even when they expire before the death of the donor. Planned giving tends to be far more transformative than spot giving.
- *O*pportunity giving occurs when a person makes a large contribution to fund a project. Opportunity giving is a subcategory of Gottlieb's problem-solving donations in which the problem being solved is of a significant scale, such as underwriting the cost of a building or a laboratory within a building or providing the funds to support a long-term research project.

  The "opportunity" involved in this category of giving is related to a proposal that the institution takes to the donor, not the donor to the institution. In this way, opportunity giving occurs when donors "avail themselves of the opportunity" to have a stadium named after them or to feel the satisfaction of eliminating a deadly disease.
- *R*eaction giving, like opportunity giving, occurs because one is asked. But its scale usually falls somewhere between spot giving and opportunity giving. It's called *reaction giving* because it's not initiated by the donors themselves but done in reaction to a solicitation made by an organization. For example, if you receive a letter from an organization that supports the welfare of animals and decide to give $500, you're making a reaction gift.

That donation is a good deal larger than the $5 you might contribute as a spot gift to a Boy Scout who knocks on your door soliciting contributions to the local animal shelter, but it's also far smaller than the $50 million planned gift or opportunity gift you might make to have a local veterinary clinic named after you.

In higher education, reaction giving often occurs as a result of outreach campaigns to parents of current students (see later) or general scholarship appeals. For these types of gifts, active solicitation is required in order to make the donor aware of an existing need and how their support may be used to help alleviate that need.

- *T*ax reduction giving occurs when a gift is structured in such a way as to provide the greatest tax advantage to the donor. When potential donors talk about their philanthropic interests, they rarely mention tax reduction as among their greatest priorities. However, in the experience of the authors, no donor of a large gift has ever rejected the tax advantages that may result from the contribution. In other words, sizable gifts often start out as planned, opportunity, or reaction giving but may sometimes turn into tax reduction giving, as the details are worked out.

In these cases, the donor should be encouraged to consult his or her own financial advisor in order to learn how best to itemize annual deductions or structure an estate in order to achieve the greatest tax advantages.

EIGHT STEPS TO SUCCESSFUL SOLICITATION

With the exception of spot giving, all the other types of donations in the SPORT of Giving require an extended cultivation process during which the fundraiser gets to know the prospective donor. Throughout this cultivation period, the college or university isn't just trying to learn the prospect's preferences and motives, but also working to bring that person into the inner circle of involvement with the institution. We can think of this process as a series of eight steps.

Step One: Performing Background Research.

Before any meeting with a prospect for a significant gift, successful academic fundraisers do their homework. They learn what they can about the prospect's giving capacity, known philanthropic interests, professional history, family history, and anything else that can be gleaned from the public record. Development professionals are quite familiar with the fundamental strategies of prospect research. They use fundraising databases, Internet searches, media outlets (including professional magazines and society pages that academic administrators may not be familiar with), and the personal insights that can be provided by members of the school's governing board, various advisory boards, and prior donors.

For their part, the academic administrators or faculty members who are working on the project can use their professional knowledge to help put the prospective donor's interests into an appropriate context. For example, someone might assume that knowing a prospect's father had been trained as a geographer was in itself a valuable piece of information. But the faculty members and academic administrators on the team would know that physical geography and human geography are distinct enough fields as to be almost completely different disciplines. They can help prevent others on the team from making a gaffe by misunderstanding information they'd gained from the research.

Most important of all, however, world-class fundraisers use the information resulting from their research very carefully: People like to know that the people they're interacting with from the institution have taken the time to learn a bit about them as individuals. They don't like feeling as though they're being "stalked" as a target for financial gain. They also don't like having their opportunities to talk about their accomplishments cut short by the impression that their visitors already know everything they're about to share. As a result, background information should help guide the conversations that follow; it shouldn't be the primary substance of the conversation.

Step Two: Planning the Initial Contact.

It isn't enough for fundraisers merely to know everything they can about a prospective donor. They also have to go into each of their meetings with that person aware of what the agenda will be, who will do what, at which point in the meeting it will be time to proceed to the next agenda item, when the meeting should be expected to end, and how to cut the meeting short if, for whatever reason, it doesn't go well. Most initial meetings will have a plan something like the following:

- *Pleasantries*. For the first three to five minutes, greetings are usually exchanged and typical "getting acquainted" conversations take place. If someone on the team has a friend or business associate in common with the prospective donor, this phase of the meeting offers a good time to mention that. Other topics might include the beauty of the prospect's home or office, the weather that day, a recent athletic event (if prior research indicates that the prospect likes sports), or traffic on the way to the meeting.

    Often, the development officer (DO) takes the lead during this phase of the conversation since he or she is more comfortable conversing with strangers who don't have academic backgrounds than others may be.

- *Transition.* Once pleasantries wind down—and almost all prospective donors will indicate this moment has arrived by allowing there to be a momentary lull or break in the conversation—the discussion should begin to turn to the actual purpose of the meeting. This transition is usually done by either the DO or the academic officer (AO), so it's important to agree in advance who will assume this responsibility and how it will be performed. Frequently, the member of the team thanks the prospect for taking the time from his or her busy schedule to meet with them and shares how the program they are representing is conducting important work and benefiting the community or the world.
- *Soft Proposal.* After the transition has occurred, another member of the team then describes how the program could provide even greater benefits if it were the recipient of a philanthropic gift. The soft proposal is not itself an ask: The prospective donor is never directly identified as the person who is expected to make the philanthropic gift. (He or she will connect the dots anyway. Prospective donors did not accumulate their assets by being dense.) Nor is a specific size of the anticipated gift mentioned, except possibly in very general terms.

If the initial meeting is being conducted at a restaurant, a good time to enter the soft proposal phase of the discussion is shortly after the meal order has been placed. Other members of the team can then enter the discussion to elaborate on points raised earlier during the transition and soft proposal phases. Each member of the team should try to say at least one or two things at this point. Since some members of the team will be more adept at thinking on their feet than others, the planning discussion can be used to assign talking points to specific people.

It's important to remember, however, that this is a conversation, not a PowerPoint presentation. The discussion should flow naturally, allowing the prospect to ask questions and add other information.

- *Determining Interest.* During some initial contacts, it will be obvious whether the prospect is or isn't interested in the project. Some people will state their level of interest bluntly: "This is exactly the kind of work that fascinates me" or "I've got to admit that this isn't the sort of thing I really care about." At other times, the person's facial expressions and body language will tell the fundraiser all he or she needs to know. At still other times, someone will have to ask. Usually, this responsibility is assigned to either the AO or the DO. The question will then take the form of something like the following: "Based on everything you've heard so far, is this something that you can see yourself helping us with?"

- *Moving Forward.* Since the initial contact does not contain a hard proposal or ask, it's important to wrap up the conversation with a flexible plan for the future. The team might promise to follow up with some specific information within a few days (an approach that's particularly useful if the prospect has asked questions that can't be answered at the initial meeting itself) or merely to get together again at a future date.

The goal at this point should not only be to leave the conversation completely open-ended—"So, let's do lunch again sometime."—but also be not to try to force a commitment from the prospective donor too early. He or she will have much to think about and to discuss with others, such as family members and financial advisors. An agreement to talk again in one to three weeks allows sufficient time for those conversations to take place but doesn't delay the discussion to such a point that it has to begin with the basics all over again.

Step Three: Making the Initial Contact.

Once a plan is in place, it's time to schedule the initial contact itself. The best scenario is for this meeting to be arranged by a third party. Someone who knows both the prospect and at least one member of the advancement team can suggest the meeting to the prospective donor, arrange for introductions to be made, and attend the initial contact meeting if that is possible and seems desirable.

Being physically present at the initial contact may not always be possible for the third party: He or she may live some distance away and have suggested the meeting through a phone call, letter, or e-mail message. It may also not be desirable for the third party to be present: He or she may not be comfortable in this kind of setting or may have the type of personality that would dominate the conversation.

In any case, the initial contact should always occur somewhere the prospective donor feels relaxed. In order of preference, the best locations are the prospect's home, his or her office, a restaurant, and another neutral location. One thing to keep in mind if holding the initial contact meeting at a restaurant is to request seating at a table (not a booth) in an area where you are the least likely to be disturbed by music or loud conversations. Booths can be awkward for certain people to get into and out of, and first meetings can feel awkward enough anyway without introducing this further complication. In addition, booths can be tight fits for tall or portly people, and a good fundraiser wants to do everything in his or her power to put the person at ease. (Of course, if the prospective donor says, "Oh, let's sit at a booth instead," the team always honors this request.)

Throughout the meeting, follow the plan as carefully as possible, always allowing for the unexpected to occur. The prospective donor may see someone he or she knows in the restaurant and invite that person to the table or have other family members at home whom the team did not know would be present. (For this reason, if bringing materials or gift items to share, always have a few extra.) Occasionally, a prospective donor will interrupt a carefully planned conversation to say, "Are you going to want money from me?" When that occurs, successful fundraisers are honest and say that they hope the person will want to become more engaged with the program and support it financially. But fundraisers who are truly world-class also make it clear that the purpose of that day's meeting is not to make a specific request but rather to determine the person's level of interest in the project.

Step Four: Conducting Subsequent Meetings.

After the initial contact has been made, there can be any number of subsequent meetings before the team feels that the time has come for a formal request to be made. These subsequent meetings should follow roughly the same format as the initial contact, but they should always build on the previous discussion. Although there should be a certain amount of consistency in terms of who is present at these meetings, other people may be added to the group for specific purposes.

For example, a representative of the institution's legal team might be present to discuss certain technical requirements of the potential gift, although he or she should never be presented as the donor's legal representative, but instead as serving the institution's interests. For very large gifts, the president or chair of the governing board might take part. Students or faculty members may be on hand to discuss how the project would help them. The goal of these subsequent meetings is to answer any questions the potential donor may have, build mutual trust, and develop the person's level of interest in the program.

Step Five: Planning the Ask.

At some point in the relationship, the development office will decide that the time is right to move from the soft proposal to a hard proposal: to make the ask. Timing is everything at this point. If the team makes an ask too early, the prospect can pull back because he or she may feel that the institution is being presumptuous. (Being on the receiving end of an ask made too soon feels similar to being proposed to on a first date: You don't know whether the other person is impetuous, crazy, overconfident, or all three. Spoiler alert: It's always all three.)

If the team waits too long, the prospect's interest may cool or other, more pressing needs may arise. So, the team has to be alert to the prospect's signals that the time is right to move the relationship to the next stage. Often, those signals are very obvious. In a surprising number of cases, the prospective donor comes right out and asks something like, "So, what can I do to help?"

At other times, the signals may be a bit more subtle, such as a continued high level of interest but no additional questions or suggestions as to how the project might be improved. In either case, the representatives of the institution have to plan who will make the ask, at what level the request will be, and what the backup plan will be if the prospect makes a counteroffer.

The person making the ask should be someone who is both comfortable in this situation and trusted by the prospective donor. In the vast majority of cases, that person will be the DO but there are situations in which an AO is sufficiently experienced in fundraising and close enough to the donor to be the logical person to make the ask. The level at which the request is made should be justifiable in terms of the fundraising goal and the budget that will be required. The worst possible answer to the question, "So, let's say I *do* give you twenty million dollars. What would you do with it?" is no answer at all. The school needs to have a plan ready for using the donation with enough detail to be compelling. Points that might arise are as follows:

- If it will be invested, what will the yield be?
- What will the draw (i.e., the percentage of the yield that is expended each year) be?
- How will the expendable portion be used?
- Why was that particular amount chosen?

Once the ask is made, the easiest situations are those in which the potential donor says "yes" or "no." If the person says "yes," break out the champagne. If the person says "no," he or she really means *not now*, and the team has an opportunity to reexamine its strategy for moving forward. But counteroffers pose a particular challenge. If the donor cannot fund the entire project at the amount requested, is it still worth moving forward? How will the shortfall be made up? What is the minimal acceptable amount that makes the project worth proceeding?

And who on the team is authorized to make a final decision in the name of the institution? For example, if a donor is asked for $50 million to acquire the naming rights for a new fitness facility, what do you do if he or she offers only $10 million but still requests the naming rights? That offer remains quite substantial, but someone needs to decide how the rest of the facility will be funded and if naming rights can still be offered when the gift is only one-fifth of the ask.

Step Six: Making the Ask.

When the plan has been made, a meeting with the prospective donor should then be arranged so that the formal ask can be made. The ask should be for a specific amount contributed over a specific period and is likely to require some thought on part of the prospective donors. After all, what the college or university is seeking is a transformational gift and that is something on a much different scale from a simple transfer of funds. The institution's representatives are sharing visions and dreams with the donor. There should be an air of excitement about the possibilities that are in store. At the same time, that atmosphere shouldn't be manufactured or insincere.

Instead, it should flow naturally from the five previous steps in this process so that this moment seems the logical culmination of all previous conversations. The ask should never be unexpected by the donor, even though he or she may not be aware of the precise amount and details of the request. If there ever is a donor who is surprised by being asked for money at this point in the process, the fundraisers have not done their cultivation properly.

Step Seven: Being Quiet.

Once the ask has been made, the best (but also the hardest) thing for those representing the institution to do is simply to remain silent. Give the prospect time to consider everything that has been presented and discussed. It will seem natural to want to fill the silence that often results as the person is thinking over what the team has said, but it's the prospect's role to break the silence that can result after the ask, not the role of the team members.

When responses occur, they can be almost anything. What you hope for, of course, is that the person will say that he or she would be happy to help you out in this way. But although that type of complete agreement does occur, it doesn't occur very often. More frequently, the donor will eventually say that he or she will have to talk the matter over with a spouse, another family member, lawyer, or financial advisor. There are also other common statements the donor might make at this point, and an effective fundraiser needs to be ready for them. (See Figure 4.1.)

The goal is, thus, to keep the conversation going until a gift agreement of some acceptable form is reached. (An exception is, of course, if the prospective donor makes it clear that he or she can't or won't support the project. Then, as we saw in Chapter 3, it's unethical and unwise to press the issue.) If further discussions are to be held, the representatives of the school should try to set a date and time for the next meeting before leaving the conversation.

If the prospective donor says:	A member of the team might respond:
"I need more time to think about this."	*"Is there additional information that we may provide to help you make your decision?"*
"Give me a month to consider this."	*"Let's set a date to meet again."*
"This is quite a sum you are asking."	*"This is an important project, and we believe this level of leadership is needed in order to achieve the ambitious goals we've been discussing with you."*
"I can't make this kind of gift right now."	*"Is it the timing of the gift or the amount that concerns you?" (The answer to this question will suggest the next course of action to follow.)*
"The amount is too large."	*"What amount do you feel comfortable committing?"*
"My current finances won't make a gift of this size possible until date."	*"Cen we get your commitment to reconsider this request in a year's time then?"*
"I need to meet with my accountant and financial advisor."	*"We'd be pleased to go with you and meet with your advisors with your permission to answer any questions they many have and to clarify our expected processes and procedures."*
"I can't give $XXX, but I will give you $YYY."	*"Although $YYY won't cover the anticipated expenses of the project we've outlined, could you make that level of gift now and then add to it next year?"*
"I already made a commitment to XYZ organization that I'm obliged to complete, and that will take two more years."	*"In that case, are you willing to make a commitment now with the payments to begin in two years?" (If the person agrees, the team can them ask the person for a bridge payment to help cover operating expenses over the next two years.)*

Figure 4.1   Common Statements the Donor Might Make.

Step Eight: Stewarding the Gift.

The last line of Aristotle's *Nicomachean Ethics* is, "Now let's begin." The idea is that, since Aristotle regarded ethics as inseparable from the social context in which people operated, everything he had said about ethics really couldn't be fully applied until the reader had examined his following work: the *Politics*. The solicitation process is much the same.

Once the donor has made his or her commitment, the fundraiser's work has only just begun. There will be many technical details to address as the gift is received and booked, and then the whole process of responsible stewardship comes into play. World-class fundraisers don't regard their work as over once a gift is received; they regard it as just beginning.

For other approaches to characterizing the donor "life cycle," see Polivy, 2013.

THE ACID TEST

Obviously, it takes a lot of time to follow all eight of these development steps with a donor. Experienced fundraisers know that they can't afford to devote that much effort to everyone. That's why one activity they engage in during their moves meetings or strategy sessions is potential donor triage. Which of their prospects fall into each of the following categories?

- Those who have a high probability of making a contribution in the very near future. These are the prospects the institution wants to solicit.
- Those who are likely to make a contribution at some point, but not immediately. These are the prospects the institution wants to cultivate.
- Those who may or may not make a contribution at some point. These are the prospects the institution wants to study.
- Those who are highly unlikely to make a contribution. These are the prospects the institution wants to reclassify (perhaps as community supporters or friends of the university rather than as potential donors).

But how is this type of triage conducted? What criteria do you use to assign your various prospects to different categories? One systematic way of classifying potential donors is to see which of them pass the *ACID Test*.

- *A* is for *A*bility. What is the person's capacity to make a gift at the level under consideration?
- *C* is for *C*ontact with the institution. What is the person's level of engagement with the institution or program?

- *I* is for *I*nterest. How much enthusiasm has the person had for the project or proposal in the past?
- *D* is for *D*esire. How ready does the person appear to be to make a philanthropic gift at this moment in his or her life?

The four components of the ACID test illustrate why there is such a poor return on cold calls: The institution doesn't know the person's ability to give, hasn't had any past contact with the person, hasn't made any efforts to develop the person's interest in the proposal, and has no information about the person's desire to contribute at this time.

There's a certain amount of subjectivity that inevitably becomes involved in the ACID test. You can't always be aware of what's going through another person's mind, even when that person has always appeared to be engaged when you've discussed the project and its possibilities. Although you can't eliminate that subjectivity, you can help reduce it by applying the ACID test consistently and systematically through use of the following form: (See Figure 4.2.)

You can also customize this matrix according to your own experience and the project you're currently working on. For example, suppose that experience has demonstrated that, for the pool of prospects you deal with, ability and contact are less informative as criteria than are interest and desire. You can adjust the weights upward or downward as long as the highest possible score remains 100. In the example we just gave, if ability and contact are each weighted 3, and interest and desire are each weighted 7, the maximum score remains the same but an individual prospect's score will change to reflect your own personal experience.

In much the same way, you can adjust scores on the prospect rating matrix to reflect the nature of the project you're working on. With the default weights in place, it's possible for a prospect who's capable of making a $2,500 gift to receive the same score as a prospect who's capable of making a $5 million gift. If the project you're working on is a capital campaign, the latter gift could assume even more importance than it would ordinarily have: It may be the difference between being able to say whether the campaign was a success or a failure.

For this reason, you may want to assign a weight of 11 to ability, reducing the weight of the other three criteria to 3 each. The resulting scores will, thus, be more appropriate for the specific project you're working on. (For a variety of other approaches to quantifying and measuring the success of fundraising strategies, see Hager, 2003.)

PROSPECT RATING FOR_____*(name of prospect)*			
CRITERIA	RANK: 1 lowest – 5 highest	X WEIGHT	EQUALS SCORE
Ability		5	
Contact with institution		5	
Interest		5	
Desire at this time		5	
Total score			
Interpreting the score			
> 90	Solicit: What are you waiting for?		
80–90	Cultivate: This appears to be strong candidate for making a gift. Continue to develop a relationship for the next six to twelve months and then reevaluate. Then ask again within six to twelve months.		
70–80	Study: Try to ascertain the person's readiness for giving, perhaps by soliciting a smaller gift or a contribution to the annual fund. If that is successful, continue building the relationship for another eighteen months to two years and then reevaluate.		
> 70	Reclassify: If you've been working with this prospect for at least a year, consider this person to be a goodwill ambassador for the institution or program instead of a potential donor. If the relationship has not yet lasted a year, invest a bit more time, focusing on the criteria that you scored the lowest, then reevaluate.		

Figure 4.2   Prospect Rating Matrix.

CASE STUDY

For nearly two years, a department chair, a DO, and the department's business manager have been getting together with the head of Acme Coyote Supply Company, an international conglomerate based near their institution, with the goal of securing sufficient funding to endow a named professorship in the chair's discipline. Although it is always the institution that reaches out to the company and not vice versa, the president of Acme is never less than delighted to see them and has enjoyed their frequent discussions over lunch at La Table Très Chere, his favorite restaurant, as well as admission to the president's skybox at several home football games and free tickets to the university's annual gala.

What has been more difficult, however, has been trying to determine what this prospective donor's role might be in the institution's fundraising activities. Whenever the DO began to speak about programs in the department chair's discipline, the Acme president kept redirecting the discussion toward athletics. Whenever the discussion went on for more than a few minutes about athletics, the prospective donor would talk about a recent movie or television show.

Each time the chair, DO, and business manager would drive back from one of these lunches, they would find themselves baffled over what the prospective donor really cared about. They kept running into obstacles any time they got too close to the subject that really brought them all together: the endowed professorship. Every time members of the team contacted the prospect's secretary to arrange a date and time for the next lunch, their hopes began to rise, only to be dashed again by another meeting that seemed to go nowhere.

Seeking to move the discussion forward, they tried a number of different approaches. For example, they took the Acme president several proposals in which the endowed professorship was configured in different ways; the prospect put them off saying that such an important matter would require time for study and reflection. When they asked about the proposals again at a lunch a few weeks later, the prospect had "inadvertently" left the documents behind in the office.

At the next lunch, when the same excuse about accidentally leaving the documents behind came up, the DO handed the prospect extra copies; the response this time was that this discussion really should take place sometime when the president, provost, and board chair were all present so that they could discuss which concept fit best into the school's strategic plan. The chair and DO then arranged a lunch with the prospective donor and a select group of university stakeholders: the president, provost, board chair, several faculty members, a few students, and other donors—everyone they could think of who might have an important prospective on this project. The Acme president deflected every question people posed, with other questions about their lives, their goals, the areas of their research, and plenty of other matters that moved further and further from the topic of the endowed position.

When the last event was over, the chair had had enough. "I really don't have time to keep doing this. I don't think Acme Coyote Supply Company is ever going to give us a donation, at least not one that's worth the investment we've already made. I think the president just likes talking and being treated to lunch. I'm pulling the plug on this effort."

Question: Is the department chair right to give up at this point?

Possible Strategies

Some potential donors are seriously interested in making a contribution that will help move a program or institution forward; they're goal oriented. Others just seem to enjoy the attention they receive from being courted by the institution; they're process oriented. The three important questions for academic fundraisers to ask themselves at this point are:

1. Is it realistic to assume that we can move this process closer to the goal we have in mind?
2. Would doing so be worth the investment we have to make in terms of time, effort, and other resources?
3. Would doing so be in keeping with sound practice and ethical principles (the topics we discussed in Chapter 2)?

The three members of the fundraising team in this story find themselves at a point where they are wondering whether they can answer the first question affirmatively. Indeed, the department chair has already decided that the answers to both of the first two questions must be "no." The issue is whether the other members of the group should concur.

This situation might be one in which each member of the group completes a prospect rating sheet and then compares his or her answers with the others in order to determine how well the Acme president does on the ACID test. If we retain the default weights assigned to each area, one likely outcome is the following:

Ability: The president certainly has the resources to endow the position. That, after all, was the reason why the institution reached out to the prospect in the first place. Consensus answer: 5.

Contact: The case says that it was the institution that made the first contact with the prospective donor and that representatives of the institution are always the ones who take the initiative in scheduling the next lunch. It would appear, therefore, that the prospective donor has little contact with the institution unless the institution itself offers an invitation. Consensus answer: 1.

Interest: The Acme president certainly seems interested enough in issues related to the discipline to talk about them over lunch. On the other hand, the prospect seems to be interested in a lot of different things, so the conversation rarely stays on any one topic for more than a few minutes. Consensus answer: 3.

Desire: The prospect has used every excuse imaginable to defer making a decision—or even to be seriously asked—about a major gift. The desire seems to be for attention, expensive lunches, and perks such as invitations to the skybox at the football stadium, not to be a serious partner in moving this project forward. Consensus answer: 1.

Total Score on the ACID Test: $(5 + 1 + 3 + 1 = 10)$ x $5 = 50$.

Since any score below 70 on the ACID test falls into the *reclassify* category, the school is probably wise to scale back its efforts in trying to cultivate the president of Acme Coyote Supply Company. The prospect can still be kept on the mailing list for public events, but the strategy of scheduling regular lunches appears to be pointless to continue, just as the department chair concluded. It's possible that, after having received so much attention for nearly two years, the prospective donor may miss the attention and reach out to the institution. If that happens, the Contact score on the ACID test might increase enough to warrant further study. But the institution should make it clear, as diplomatically as possible, that the school's needs are so great that it can only devote a limited amount of time to non-donors.

CONCLUDING THOUGHTS

Cultivating donors and soliciting major gifts take time. Dividing tasks among various representatives of the school is, thus, to everyone's advantage. The DO can take the lead in meeting the prospective donor's expectations for social engagement. The AO can take the lead in keeping the focus of the relationship on the institution or academic program. Students and faculty members can help give the project a human face. Lawyers can make sure that all legal requirements are met. Public relations specialists can make sure that events receive the attention they deserve, and so on.

Moreover, when any one member of the team is otherwise occupied, there are plenty of people who can step in to make the donor feel sufficiently appreciated and attended to. Using the SPORT of giving and ACID test techniques, the development staff can effectively triage situations so that it's devoting its energy to opportunities where it'll have the greatest impact. That's the secret to the success enjoyed by world-class fundraisers as well as to the source of their popularity with the donors who helped them succeed.

REFERENCES

Gottlieb, H. (2008). *The Pollyanna principles: Reinventing* "nonprofit organizations" to create the future of our world. Tucson, AZ: Renaissance Press.

Hager, M. A. (Ed.) (2003). *Exploring measurement and evaluation efforts in fundraising*. San Francisco, CA: Jossey-Bass.

Polivy, D. K. (2013). *Donor cultivation and the donor lifecycle map: A new framework for fundraising*. Hoboken, NJ: Wiley.

RESOURCES

Joyaux, S. P. (2011). *Strategic fund development: Building profitable relationships that last*. (3rd Ed.) Hoboken, NJ: Wiley.

Sturtevant, W. T. (2004). *The artful journey: Cultivating and soliciting the major gift*. Chicago: Institutions Press.

Chapter Five

Raising Awareness, Not Just Money

If there's a single sentiment that academic leaders hear repeatedly from the fundraisers at their institutions, it's that development professionals aren't just in the fundraising business; they're also in the friend-raising business. It's our experience that academic leaders may smile politely when they hear this oft-repeated platitude, but inwardly they're probably wincing that anyone would think that any sentiment that corny could possibly be true. And yet the fact of the matter remains that anyone involved in development can't devote all his or her time to raising money for the programs they support. Academic fundraisers must also play a key role in raising the public awareness of those programs.

If receiving philanthropic gifts is the end that most people think of when they're talking about fundraising, increasing awareness and community engagement are the means. Unless a very small amount is involved, a prospective donor will want to know about an organization before he or she is willing to contribute to it.

For a college or university, that knowledge may come from being a student, alumnus, parent, business partner, interested member of the community, or in some other way. But how can successful fundraisers increase the likelihood that the right people get the right information about the programs they're responsible for? In this chapter, we explore a few best practices in how academic and advancement professionals can work together to improve public awareness of an institution and then to build that awareness into positive community engagement.

IDENTITY

Before anyone else can know who you are, you have to know it. You have to have a clear sense of your program's identity, service region, purpose, primary stakeholder groups, and trajectory. At first, many readers might think, "But that's easy. We have a mission statement." Mission statements are certainly important, and we encouraged you in Chapter 3 to be sure that you developed an adequate mission statement for any volunteer board associated with your team. But the mission statements of institutions and programs are a little different: As public statements, they often try to contain language that will appeal to every possible stakeholder group and, for this reason, tend to become overly general. They're actually not particularly helpful in answering the key question related to your identity: How are we in this unit different from other units with similar names at other institutions? Or how are we at this institution different from other colleges or universities that are generally viewed as our peers?

A mission statement is often too long to provide clear answers to those questions. So, what any academic fundraiser needs to do is to be able to express the identity of the unit or program that he or she serves in a single sentence structured as follows: (See Textbox 5.1.)

Let's consider a few ways in which that type of identity statement—an expression we'll use to distinguish it from a mission statement—might develop for different types of programs and schools.

- What drives us at Cost Conscious Community College is our strong commitment to provide access to meaningful careers to first-generation college students and other nontraditional learners in the southwest quadrant of our state, and so our most important goal for the future is building strong ties with local industry for internships and job placement.
- What drives us at Exclusive Private University's medical school is our strong commitment to prepare world-class physicians of tomorrow for research at major international universities and leadership positions at the world's finest hospitals in an effort that's unbounded by geography, and so our most important goal for the future is building a new cardiac wing that's second to none.
- What drives us at Centrally Located State University's College of Arts and Letters is our strong commitment to improve the communication and

---

What drives us at [NAME OF UNIT OR INSTITUTION] is our strong commitment to [VERB SPECIFYING YOUR AREA'S PURPOSE] to/or [NOUN SPECIFYING PRIMARY STATEHOLDER GROUP] in [PLACE SPECIFYING PRIMARY SERVICE REGION], and so our most important goal for the future is [PHRASE SPECIFYING A SINGLE OVERARCHING GOAL].

critical thinking skills for undergraduate and graduate students who hail from the heartland of Eastern West Dakota, and so our most important goal for the future is hiring additional faculty with a student-centered, learning-focused philosophy.

When you read the mission statements developed by many colleges, universities, and community colleges, they're so similar that it's difficult to tell them apart. (For an exercise in doing so, see Buller, 2015, 116–119.) But no one will confuse the three hypothetical institutions described earlier. As you think about the identity of the programs you serve, keep in mind the following principle: If you can't express your identity in a single sentence, your listener won't understand it even if you describe it for an hour.

BRANDING

Closely related to the concept of your program's identity is its *brand*. Faculty members and administrators on the academic side of the university often bristle at the idea that their institution, college, or department has a "brand." They identify this term with the corporate world, associating it with salesmen, even hucksters, and feel it has no place in the world of higher education.

One lesson in diplomacy that academic fundraisers quickly learn is that there's no point in using a vocabulary that makes a stakeholder uncomfortable. If people shudder at the notion of including a certain organization in their wills, a successful fundraiser will speak instead of planned giving or charitable trusts, avoiding words like *will, bequest*, and *death*.

Similarly, if faculty members don't care for the idea of branding, the development officers (DOs) at that institution will simply speak with them in terms of the program's distinctive features, reputation, and mission. But you, at least, as someone who aspires to become a world-class academic fundraiser, should understand the concept of these euphemisms. It's a matter of branding the program you represent and being able to represent that brand effectively to members of the community.

Every institution—and each program within that institution—has a unique brand. That brand may not be very strong in some cases, but it will still be present. The brand is the set of symbols that differentiates one institution or program from another. For the institution, officially established school colors, logos, a mascot, a team name, distinctive works of architecture, and other immediately recognizable visual symbols are all part of its brand.

But words and expressions can be part of a brand as well. The expression "between the hedges" is part of the University of Georgia's brand because of the privet hedges that stand on each side of Sanford Field. "The Golden Dome" is part of the University of Notre Dame's brand because of the gilded dome atop its main building; students and alumni of the institution often casually refer to themselves as "domers," another verbal ingredient in Notre Dame's brand. Branding can also include gestures like the Hook 'Em Horns hand signal of the University of Texas or the Gator Chomp of the University of Florida.

Finally, branding can include traditions like the Ring Figure dance and presentation of class rings at Virginia Military Institute or the Primal Scream on the night before finals at Carleton College. Branding is part of what members of the community most closely associate with an institution or program. It provides an emotional and conceptual shortcut that can save fundraisers from having to explain to someone what a particular college or university is all about, why its work is important, and how it matters to the wider world.

For this reason, world-class fundraisers tend to rely heavily on brands as they reach out to the community. They have documents, pens, bookmarks, folders, and other giveaways prominently marked with the institution's logo. They pose for photographs (and often get members of the university to pose) using the gestures or hand signals that are associated with their school. They refer to themselves as Aggies or Sooners or Vols or whatever nickname is in common use at their school.

Taglines can also be a powerful component of the brand established by an institute or a program. A tagline is a phrase so commonly associated with an organization that, as soon as you hear those words, you think of that organization. Businesses have long known the power of taglines. As an exercise, the following is a list of taglines, some of which have not even been used for several decades. Nevertheless, most people will instantly recognize the company that used that tagline. (See Table 5.1.)

Table 5.1 Corporate Tagline Quiz

Instructions: See how many taglines in the left column you can match with the appropriate company in the right column.

1. Where's the beef?	a. Burger King
2. Don't leave home without it.	b. Coca Cola
3. We bring good things to life!	c. Apple Computer
4. Snap! Crackle! Pop!	d. Johnson's Baby Shampoo
5. No more tears.	e. McDonalds
6. It's the real thing.	f. Avis
7. I'm lovin' it!	g. General Electric
8. Have it your way.	h. American Express
9. We try harder.	i. Kellogg's Rice Krispies
10. Think different.	j. Wendy's

Answers: 1. j, 2. h, 3. g, 4. i, 5. d, 6. b, 7. e, 8. a, 9. f, 10. c. Those taglines are so closely associated with their companies that some readers will find them easy to identify, even though these expressions may have been dropped from advertising campaigns before they were born. That's the power of a good tagline: It continues to have an emotional impact and advertising value even when it's no longer in current use.

Colleges and universities also have taglines, although few of them are as familiar as the slogans used by nationally advertised products. The following is a list of taglines—some of them current, others now retired—from major U.S. universities. Most people find these taglines rather challenging to associate with the institutions that developed them. (See Table 5.2.)

Answers: 1. d, 2. i, 3. a, 4. j, 5. g, 6. b, 7. c, 8. f, 9. e, 10. h. One reason why these taglines are more difficult to identify with their institutions is that very few colleges and universities have the type of national advertising budget that major corporations do. As a result, we simply hear corporate slogans more frequently than we do academic slogans. Another reason why corporate and university taglines tend to be different is that it's often easier to differentiate products than programs.

Certainly, the experience of a student at a Great Books institution like St. John's College is not at all comparable to that of a student at a focused professional school like the Savannah College of Art and Design. Nevertheless, to many of those outside of academia, those two experiences seem much more alike than do, for example, a soft drink and an automobile. The ability to highlight not just the distinctive nature of this particular product but also the distinctive nature of this whole class of products vis-à-vis others gives commercial taglines a definite advantage.

Table 5.2 Academic Tagline Quiz

Instructions: See how many taglines in the left column you can match with the appropriate institution in the right column.

1. Forward. Thinking.	a. University of Minnesota.
2. Grasp the forces driving the change.	b. The Ohio State University.
3. Only at the U.	c. Mary Baldwin University.
4. Knowledge to go places.	d. University of Wisconsin.
5. Advancing knowledge. Transforming lives.	e. California State University, Los Angeles.
6. Do something great.	f. University of Nebraska.
7. Taking your success personally.	g. Michigan State University.
8. Pioneering new frontiers.	h. University of Texas at Austin.
9. Where great futures begin	i. Stanford University.
10. What starts here changes the world.	j. Colorado State University.

Third, and perhaps more important, the large budgets than many corporations have at their disposal mean that companies can afford to hire the best advertising firms available, which often produce clearly superior results. No one will deny that a tagline like "Think different." has an edge over "Grasp the forces driving the change." in terms of being pithy and memorable. Slogans tend to be one of those commodities where you get what you pay for, and those who can afford to pay more usually get far more distinctive taglines.

None of the preceding reservations should lead us to conclude, however, that taglines can't be an important component of community relations for colleges and universities. Taglines simply continue the process of refining a mission statement into an identity statement, an identity statement into an elevator speech (a ten- or fifteen-second pitch for a program that answers the question, "What would I tell someone about what we do if we were together for only the duration of a brief elevator ride?"), and an elevator speech into a slogan or motto.

Informal taglines can be developed during a strategy session or retreat in which representatives of the institution work collaboratively to determine how the programs they represent are different from (or better, superior to) others. (For some ideas on how to conduct this type of exercise, see Buller, 2016, 63–64.)

More formal taglines are best developed by public relations or advertising professionals who are trained in how to craft these statements effectively. After all, you want your tagline to be more like the fast food chain Carl's Jr.'s "Eat like you mean it" than its earlier "If it doesn't get all over the place, it doesn't belong in your face," which is frequently ridiculed as one of the worst slogans in advertising history. (See, for example, my.xfinity.com/slideshow/news-worstfastfoodslogans/2/, www.cracked.com/blog/the-7-worst-slogans-in-history-advertising/, and www.ruethedayblog.com/2008/06/the-worlds-8-worst-slogans-ever/.)

EXPERT DATABASES AND SPEAKERS BUREAUS

A college or university is, due its very nature, a place where experts in many different areas are gathered. Your institution's external stakeholders regularly need experts on various topics.

- The local newspaper might want someone to provide an informed opinion about critical issues in an upcoming election.
- A service organization might need a speaker who can provide a background about a conflict going on somewhere in the world.

• A community organization might have a number of residents on the verge of retirement who want an unbiased view about what type of investments to retain for the future, when to begin drawing on their Social Security benefits, and what type of Medicare supplemental insurance to purchase for their individual needs.

Colleges and universities have faculty members with expertise in all of these areas, and making that expertise available to a broader audience can be a wonderful way to engage with the community.

Faculty members can become involved in community engagement through an expert database (a list of specialists in various areas and their contact information so that they can be consulted when an issue related to their field arises), a speakers bureau (a list of faculty members who are willing to speak to groups about various topics, their contact information, and brief biographies), or some combination of the two.

In addition to service organizations and local schools, professional organizations sometimes make use of an institution's expert database or speakers bureau when they're looking for people to deliver a keynote address at a conference in the area. All of these opportunities allow the office of development or the public relations staff to work with the faculty expert in order to help transform, for example, a presentation on recent developments in neuroscience into a platform for introducing community members to the wider impact of the institution on their lives.

AFFINITY TRAVEL PROGRAMS

The term *affinity travel* is used to describe trips that are planned for any group sharing a common interest. Examples of affinity travel might include a music society that travels to New York in order to attend several operas and musicals, an athletic club that visits the Rose Bowl or Kentucky Derby, and an historical society that explores Gettysburg and other Civil War sites.

In higher education, affinity travel could involve a trip arranged by a certain department, program, college, or even the institution as a whole in order to visit a location that has a clear cultural or intellectual importance to the group sponsoring the trip. Designed in this way, affinity travel can be an important approach to community engagement. It can also open a new revenue stream for the program(s) offering the trip.

Those two goals—community engagement and fundraising—are nearly inseparable when it comes to affinity travel. Indeed, the value of this type of experience affects both the community and the institution on several different levels.

- Most academic affinity travel involves mixed groups of current students, parents, faculty members, alumni, community supporters, and current or potential donors. That mixture of participants results in a chemistry that can be of great benefit to the college or university hosting the trip.

  For instance, alumni can reconnect with their department or college by getting reacquainted with some of their favorite faculty members in an informal setting and by meeting the students who are continuing their traditions. Donors and potential donors meet some of the people who have benefited from (or could potentially benefit from) their generosity. Parents have the opportunity to share a unique educational and cultural experience with their children. And community supporters receive the chance to interact with a broad cross-section of individuals who are connected in some way with their own academic or cultural interests.

- Affinity travel can be an important development opportunity for institutions. After all, people who have close ties to a program are often willing to pay a premium for the opportunity to travel with the chair, dean, or president. In addition, prolonged trips provide members of the school with repeated chances to talk to community supporters and donors at length in intellectually stimulating locales. On a one- or two-week trip, academic leaders have all the time they need to present their vision of their program's future to the very people whose resources can help make that dream a reality.

  Then, after they return home, they have a compelling reason to follow up on discussions with their fellow travelers. "I was just going through my photographs, and I came across this great picture of you in front of the Louvre. I thought I'd send it to you, along with my invitation to get together for that lunch we talked about during the trip." Finally, a well-planned and organized affinity trip will leave participants with both warm memories and a strongly positive impression of your program for making those memories possible.

  Administrators discover that they have common experiences to share with others during future encounters, and the trip itself can considerably shorten the time it takes to turn a friend into a donor.

- A program's affinity travel easily generates positive publicity. In institutional publications, the local newspaper, and media outlets near the homes of the trip's participants, the experience provides a "media hook" on a topic that is exciting and beneficial for all concerned. You could focus your trip on improving international understanding, building cultural opportunities for your students, providing practical and hands-on experiences that go far beyond the textbook, or some other academic goal that is significant to your program.

The nature of the trip as an enjoyable and academic experience—as well as an opportunity that costs your institution nothing but brings it many benefits—can be reiterated in all media discussions of this program.

There are many different ways for a college or university to initiate an affinity travel program. Travel agencies and academic travel companies can handle all of the planning for a trip, and initiating an affinity travel program in this way requires little more than a telephone call. This approach may be the best alternative if you've never planned a group trip of this kind earlier and have no one on your staff who can be responsible for planning all the details. Working through an agency in this way does come at a cost, however, and it is likely that you will need to price your trip somewhat higher than if you had made the arrangements yourself.

For certain institutions or in certain markets, cost might not be a significant factor; whereas in other situations, this added cost can dissuade so many people that the trip proves not to be viable. The most cost-effective approach is to choose a destination where you or a member of your staff has a great deal of professional expertise, negotiate rates directly with hotels and bus companies, and purchase discounted blocks of tickets directly from the airline. You or members of your staff will need to plan the daily itinerary very carefully, and this task can be extremely challenging if you've never done it before. On the other hand, the process will begin to seem somewhat familiar if you've ever been responsible for planning a large conference or a two-week workshop on your home campus.

An intermediate solution is to allow a travel agency to negotiate with the hotels and transportation companies but to design the itinerary yourself. If you choose this option, it's often helpful to specify that you'd like the travel agency to provide you with their best per-person cost and that your institution will collect individual payments from the travelers, issuing a single check to the travel agency by their deadline.

This approach gives you the greatest flexibility over your pricing. Suppose, for instance, that the travel agency says that their best cost for the trip will be $2,785, based on a group size of twenty to forty participants. You might price your trip as follows:

- For every ten participants, you would like to have your expenses or those of a staff member covered. Each participant will, thus, need to be charged an additional $278.50.
- You would like each traveler to contribute $750 to your program's Annual Fund as a "premium" for participating in this special group.
- You decide to build in an extra $50 to cover the cost of special mailings, a tote bag with your program's logo, and a CD-ROM of photos after the trip

is over. That brings the cost per person to $3,863.50 ($2,785 + $278.50 + $750 + $50).

• Round this amount to $3,950 per person that your program will charge participants. The extra amount will serve as a cushion against unforeseen increases, unexpected charges, or extra treats and surprises you can provide for your guests along the way.

Priced in this way, the trip now offers you a lot of options. If twenty paying travelers sign up, you will be certain that all of your costs are covered. If all forty seats are taken, you have the option of adding an additional staff member for each ten travelers or increasing the benefit received by your Annual Fund. Just be sure that you have enough staff members along on the trip so that each traveler will feel well tended to but not so many that people feel they never have any time to themselves. Keep in mind, too, the following general guidelines for academic affinity travel:

• Specialized, domestic trips can be as short as you like, even a single day. Overseas trips, however, are best when they are between ten and fourteen days. Any shorter trip and the added cost your program will impose will make the trip seem excessively costly for the duration involved. Any longer trip will result in people having a difficult time working it into their schedule.
• Although many academic affinity trips are conducted in the summer, don't overlook the possibility of trips between terms or during spring break.
• You can frequently develop a more innovative itinerary if you work with a travel company that specializes in one particular country or region than if you work with a travel company that books trips anywhere. A more specialized travel experience often enables these companies to provide unique features to your trip that wouldn't be available to the travelers if they were to book a similar package independently.
• Handling the expenses for the trip will probably require an agency or custodial account that makes it possible for you to pass expenses through from the participants to the airlines, hotels, and the like. Your business manager or business office will need to set up this account for you and, at many institutions, a surcharge is automatically imposed on the cost. These surcharges can have a dramatic impact on the affordability of the trip.
• Don't be too greedy with the Annual Fund surcharge that you build into your trip. In most cases, $250–$750 is best. A good rule of thumb is that it's better to price a trip too low and have lots of travelers paying a small premium than to price a trip too high and have no one sign up.
• Choose your destinations carefully. Where would people most likely want to travel with a group rather than as individuals? Which destinations make

perfect sense for the mission of your unit? Which parts of the world are the most closely associated with the specialties of your faculty? What ethnic connections does the president, dean, or department chair have that might make a particular location appropriate for your trip?

- Once your expenses for the trip are clear, have the development office prepare individual letters for each traveler specifying the amount of the payment that was a contribution without consideration received. These letters will not only provide the participant with a statement that he or she can use when itemizing charitable deductions on an income tax return but also avoid any misunderstanding later about how much of the payment covered services and expenses and how much constituted a donation.

Academic affinity travel works best when you are creative in your destination and itinerary and have a compelling reason why those with an interest in your program would want to travel to that particular location. Although for you the trip will definitely be a working vacation, not simply an opportunity for you to travel for free, affinity travel provides excellent benefits for nearly any level of academic unit, with very few risks or disadvantages.

OPEN HOUSES

Institutions regularly hold open houses (sometimes known as campus visit days) for prospective students. But similar events intended for the general public can have an important development and community engagement function as well. Those involved in development can encourage the units they serve to host a series of open house events several times during the year and use those events as an opportunity to share what students and faculty members do at the institution and how they do it. One useful way to conduct an open house event is to begin with an opening session structured as follows:

a. Introduction and welcome by someone who will serve as the emcee for the event. This person should be either a DO or a lower-ranking member of the administration so that, after introducing themselves, they can give a more formal and complete introduction of the administrator who will speak next.
b. Remarks by an administrator who serves as the public image of the program or institution and who holds a higher rank than the person who made the introduction or welcome. For example, if the person who speaks in section (a) is a DO or department chair, the person who speaks in section (b) could be the president or a dean. In this section of the program, the

speaker describes the mission and vision of the institution or program and then hands the program back to the person who spoke in section (a).

c. The emcee then introduces one or more members of the faculty. If the faculty members who will speak are particularly distinguished (e.g., Nobel laureates or people who have recently been featured in the media), then up to three faculty members can be introduced. If not, it is often best to limit the faculty section of this program to a single speaker. Even the most dynamic and charismatic faculty member can cause the program to drag if the faculty section goes on for too long.

d. Brief remarks are made by faculty, with the final speaker returning the program to the emcee.

e. The emcee then introduces one or more students in the program. The students should be carefully chosen and well rehearsed. Their stories need to be compelling and have a tight structure that makes it easy for visitors to follow. They should be cautioned about using technical terms that the general public may not understand. Most community groups find student stories particularly interesting if the student had to overcome hardships in order to succeed at the school, had a level of success that is clearly remarkable (such as getting accepted into Harvard Medical School or publishing several peer-reviewed articles in top-tier journals as an undergraduate), or both. Community audiences also like to hear from students with multiple levels of success, such as the medical student who's also a concert violinist or the engineering student who's already started a private company.

f. A presentation is made by the student(s).

g. The emcee then invites the participants to engage in subsequent open house activities, such as a campus tour, a chance to sit in on a class, or a visit to an impressive laboratory or art studio.

h. The participants then reconvene for a closing reception and an opportunity to mingle with the speakers in the program and other students and faculty members.

i. If the community engagement event is also intended to have an immediate connection to fundraising, a volunteer from the community can then go to the microphone to make a pledge or gift and encourage others to do the same.

j. The emcee then thanks everyone for coming, invites the visitors to stay longer if they wish, and then closes the formal part of the program.

Open house events help increase community awareness about the full range of impact that the institution has in the area. They expose new visitors to the campus, to its offerings, and to various representatives of the institution who can then follow up with them. Open houses make it clear that your program offers hope, wonder, and discovery and that the academic and development staff work collegially to establish and strengthen relationships with members of the community. In keeping with the principles of the ACID test discussed in Chapter 4, a well-designed open house can help build the I (interest) and C (connection) that leads to successful community engagement and, in time, effective fundraising.

EDUCATIONAL AND CULTURAL ENRICHMENT

Colleges and universities regularly host a large number of lectures, concerts, performances, and other activities that can be of interest to members of the community. Although it's common for these events to be open to the public, many schools don't take full advantage of the benefits that educational and cultural programming can bring to its community engagement efforts. Just inviting people through a mass mailing or adding "Open to the public" to a poster isn't enough.

Since world-class fundraisers take the time to get to know not just established donors but also prospective donors in the community, they are aware of who would prefer to attend a jazz festival versus a performance of Brahms' *Requiem*, a lecture on the cerebral cortex versus the latest work by a controversial performance artist, and a session on how people can reduce their tax liability versus a film on relief efforts in Angola. That knowledge enables academic fundraisers to make personal invitations to those in the community who are the most likely to attend—and enjoy attending—specific types of events.

In addition to those educational and cultural events that already occur, innovative fundraisers might want to consider developing other activities that are specifically intended for members of the community. A morning coffee or an afternoon tea could highlight one professor's recent research and then open the floor for discussion.

At those events, the speaker could be introduced by a high-ranking administrator (who, it should be noted, must be comfortable and skilled in this role) who later wraps up the event at an appropriate time and provides a few insights into the work of the institution or program. In general, these events work best when they're not made open to anyone who wishes to come but are designed for a specially invited set of guests who are asked to RSVP and provide contact information so that someone from the institution can follow up with that person after the event.

By increasing awareness of what the students and faculty of a college or university are accomplishing, effective fundraisers turn community members into friends and friends into supporters. If the activity leaves the visitor with a pleasant enough experience to tell others about, it soon occurs that additional members of the community will be contacting you with requests for invitations to events and thus increasing your pool of potential friends and supporters.

SOCIAL MEDIA

At least one participant in each major fundraising project should be someone who is very familiar with social media and its latest developments. Staying current in this field is essential. Today's hot new application or website becomes tomorrow's old news. You don't want to be relying on one social media outlet when your most important stakeholders are receiving their information from another. In many cases, a student worker or volunteer can be charged with both representing the institution at public events and keeping the group up to date on what's popular and what's passé in the field of social media.

Tools such as Hootsuite and Everypost can help you manage your flow of information by posting information through multiple social media outlets, scheduling announcements in advance, and providing analytics of opening and response rates so that you can more effectively target future messages to the right audience. At regular staff meetings, people can contribute their views about which activities and achievements need to be promoted, with the student "social media czar" then crafting that message to best fit the requirements of different platforms.

Newsletters can also be an important component of a school's community engagement efforts. Print newsletters have all but disappeared, whereas online versions are burgeoning and provide a cost-effective way to reach new supporters. Regardless of the form it takes, a newsletter should be limited to the most important stories the group has, be easy to read, and appear regularly. E-mailing the newsletter is the least expensive way to distribute this information but, if doing so, remember to include an unsubscribe function in order to be compliant with spam laws.

Providing contact information for team members (usually by means of a hyperlink that automatically initiates an email message) is a common way to promote two-way communication with recipients. But remember to include at least one telephone number as well for those community members who feel more comfortable calling than writing. For that matter, it's probably a good idea for even the most technically advanced electronic newsletter to be available in print form as well, at least on demand, for readers who prefer to receive information in a more traditional format.

COMMUNITY COLLABORATION

Of course, community engagement isn't just about getting external stakeholders to come to campus. It's also about representatives of the institution going off campus, being an active part of the community, and contributing at least as much to the welfare of others as others are expected to contribute to the welfare of the institution. For this reason, almost all truly successful fundraisers are active in their communities. They belong to service organizations, help out at public events, and contribute to causes outside their colleges and universities. Whenever it's possible, they find ways of collaborating with other organizations for mutual benefit. They cosponsor trivia contests, college bowls, golf or tennis events, art and music festivals, charity walk/run races, and other activities that are appropriate for their institutions' missions.

Such activities are helpful in many different ways. They provide opportunities for members of the faculty, staff, and student body to engage with those outside their programs, benefit a worthwhile cause, and do some good for their own schools all at the same time. Moreover, by engaging in constructive activities that help the community, they serve as positive ambassadors of their programs. It's always possible that someone who's impressed by these acts of service will be the next donor, parent or grandparent of a future student, or attendee at one of the institution's public events.

A second important type of community collaboration comes in the form of service to the professional organizations that are associated with each discipline. After all, the community of a college or university isn't limited to the city or town in which the school is located. There's also a community of biologists, historians, accountants, theologians, literary critics, and every other discipline represented throughout higher education. By having faculty members and students actively involved in these associations, the institution's name is publicized and perhaps brought to the attention of those who could help support its mission.

Moreover, when students and faculty members go off to present their research at academic conferences, they might be encouraged to call on donors, alumni, and other supporters who live near the convention site. A short telephone call or visit can help reinforce the relationship that the external stakeholder has with the institution. If the person has questions or appears interested in expanding his or her involvement with the institution, someone from the school can follow up and explore new possibilities that may have gone undiscovered if it weren't for the involvement of the faculty member or student in the professional organization.

Nonprofit boards in the vicinity of the school are also important sources of community engagement. Anyone who aspires to world-class status as a fundraiser should serve on at least one of these boards. Involvement of this kind exposes the institution to people in the area who would not ordinarily come to a campus event but who might be interested in the institution's mission. It also sends the message that the college or university gives back to the community; it doesn't merely contact them when it's looking for a donation.

MEDIA AND PUBLIC RELATIONS

Regardless of its size, every college or university benefits from positive public relations. Bad publicity results in declining enrollments and contributions, whereas favorable publicity provides advertising that no amount of money can buy. If an institution—or someone who appears to be acting in the name of the institution—does something that is perceived to be disreputable, the resulting negative publicity can haunt the school for years.

In the aftermath of the Jerry Sandusky scandal at Penn State, applications dropped by 9% (about 5,000 fewer applications) and athletic donations dropped by 25% (about $8.7 million). Although the university attributed the decline to a poor economy and changing demographics, the extensive coverage of the child abuse allegations on national media could not have helped the situation. (See articles.mcall.com/2013-04-26/news/mc-penn-state-applications-down-20130426_1_university-park-lisa-powers-penn-state and deadspin.com/penn-state-athletics-donations-dropped-after-sandusky-471539461.) Mishandled public relations are difficult to recover from. They can undo decades of a development office's hard work and give donors excuses to reduce, cancel, or avoid making pledges of support.

A community relations initiative can't avoid every scandal or setback for an institution, but it can help mitigate them. The important point is not to wait until you're in the middle of a crisis to start this kind of initiative. If you pursue a community relations strategy in good times, it will already be there if you need its help during periods of negative publicity. Community boards are, thus, useful ways of getting out the message that the institution wants to focus on or amplifying the message that its professional media relations staff is conveying.

Members of the community can say things like, "What happened was terrible, and no one condones such a thing, but that isolated incident isn't reflective of the institution as a whole. In fact, if you look at how aggressively the institution dealt with the problem, I think their reaction says a lot about their values and priorities." The same argument coming from a president or dean may sound suspect and self-serving. Coming from someone who receives no financial advantage from the institution, however, that message can be tremendously compelling.

Since academic fundraisers usually work with community members who want to assist the school with its outreach efforts, the development office can help equip these volunteers by making sure that each of them has thorough knowledge of the following information:

- The tagline and elevator speech that convey the most important focus and values of the institution (or the particular program the volunteer is involved with)
- Three to five bullet points about what makes the institution or program distinctive
- Three to five bullet points that answer the question, "But what has it done for me lately?" In other words, what are some recent achievements of the institution or program that the listener should care about?

These pieces of information help equip the community member in his or her efforts to convey a positive message about the institution and its programs to others. Just as you wouldn't want to begin repairing something at your home without the right equipment, so should community volunteers not be expected to engage in a public relations initiative without the right equipment. And that equipment, in this case, is accurate and concise information.

MEDIA RELEASES

Regular press releases can be a crucial part of any school's community engagement activities. Formal press releases will almost certainly require the approval of your institution's centralized public relations or communications office. That center may even require that it be the sole source of all press releases in order to maintain consistency and prevent a less significant announcement from interfering with the attention that a major announcement issued at the same time should receive. But that shouldn't prevent innovative fundraisers from developing what we call "a media release lite" that helps get the word out about exciting events going on in the programs that the team works with.

What's the difference between a media release and a media release lite?

- A media release is an official communication from an institution about a matter it believes to be of substantial importance.
- A media release lite looks exactly like a media release, but it's unofficial and, instead of being sent to media outlets, it is sent to a carefully chosen set of internal and external stakeholders.

Suppose, for example, that a professor writes a new book or a student is presenting his or her research at an international conference. Those achievements are rarely the kind of activity that causes an institution to develop a formal press release. But they are the kind of activity that parents and students want to know about, the upper administration and governing board need to be aware of, and volunteer boards would find interesting. A media release lite sent to these constituencies (as well as the central office of public relations) informs the appropriate people about achievements in the academic program being promoted, gives the president an anecdote to drop into a speech or use in conversation with a legislator or potential donor, and assists with building a sense of pride and team spirit throughout the institution.

Since a media release lite is formatted exactly like a media release, the office of public relations can readily send it out to newspapers, radio and television stations, and bloggers if it seems important enough to them. If the document follows the same style guide that professionals use, it makes the job easier for those who are responsible for formal media releases. They don't have to start from scratch. They can simply edit the document sent to them, and their job is done. Creating these media releases lite is a good campus job or internship project for a student interested in public relations or journalism. The student can be charged with identifying and writing one positive news story every week, and then submit it to someone in the development office for revision, approval, and distribution. Each release should list a contact person and encourage the reader to follow up if he or she wants more information. If it's describing an activity directly related to fundraising, it can even contain a web address for online donations or other information about how readers can get involved in supporting that cause.

You never really know how great the impact of a media release will be. The authors were personally involved in a situation where a college benefitted significantly from a media release that wasn't specifically intended to have a fundraising connection. The release simply announced that, as the university expanded, a new college was to be formed on one of its branch campuses. A retired dentist in the area read the story in a newspaper, contacted the college, and announced that he wanted to be the new unit's very first donor. Through the combined work of academic administrators and DOs, that relationship deepened over time, and that donor eventually was responsible for helping the college obtain millions of dollars in merit scholarship support. And that whole process began with nothing more than a simple, one-paragraph media release.

AWARDS AND RECOGNITIONS

Providing awards and recognitions to members of the community results in multiple benefits to the institution. First, it links the institution's name to some positive quality that it wishes to promote. For example, the award could be for outstanding leadership, service, heroism, achievement, creativity, or perseverance. If the Winslow S. Publicfigure College of Arts and Letters annually announces the recipient of that year's Award for Outstanding Perspicacity, then over time the Winslow S. Publicfigure College of Arts and Letters will increasingly become associated with perspicacity.

It's the same phenomenon that causes Alfred Nobel to be known now mostly for physics, chemistry, medicine, literature, economics, and peace rather than dynamite, the invention from which he made his fortune. If the institution chooses to give an award that relates to a priority in its current strategic plan, it makes immediate progress in ensuring that its programs are associated with that priority in the public mind.

A second benefit from awards and recognitions is that they can prompt or solidify support from the person being honored. Colleges and universities engage in this practice all the time when they award honorary doctorates. Some of these doctorates are awarded to recognize someone's achievement or to thank them for contributions already made, whereas others are given to people from whom the institution hopes to receive a large gift.

The awards and recognitions initiated as part of an advancement effort would follow the same principle, although on a smaller scale. A prospective donor who is recognized as the recipient of the Alexandra P. Winklesworth Award for Excellence in Chirography may well be favorably inclined to make a significant gift even if he or she was hesitant earlier. The award itself comes with a fairly minimal cost. Any income that it prompts is, thus, pure revenue for the institution.

The third positive result that can arise from awards and recognitions is the opportunity for media coverage they provide. As we saw earlier, media outlets may not publicize a story about this professor's latest book or that student's conference presentation. They may well be more interested, however, when a member of the community is honored by an award.

If the presentation of the award itself is suitably impressive, television stations—which are always interested in stories that have a strong visual dimension—may be willing to cover the event. If the recipient is someone with sufficient name recognition, that coverage could even be on a regional or national scale. The only proviso to keep in mind when initiating a new award or public recognition is that an institution shouldn't have too many of them or present the same honor more than once a year.

If this activity becomes too common, it loses its impact as something rare and prestigious. For this reason, successful fundraisers try to find the right balance between having awards being few enough and rare enough to be meaningful while at the same time being common enough and presented regularly enough that they make an ongoing impact.

SELECTING MEDIA OUTLETS

Knowing where to send information for distribution is nearly as important as having good information in the first place. If the intended audience for your communication listens primarily to satellite radio and music streaming services, it does you very little good to have a story appear on National Public Radio (and vice versa). One of the advantages of having a strong commitment to community engagement and outreach is that you quickly come to know which methods of communication are the most important to which constituency.

For instance, you might learn that it's wise to choose one outlet for prospective students, another for parents, still another for legislators, and possibly even others for prospective donors. You might learn these things because you meet with different stakeholders regularly, talk to them, and find out their preferences. Community engagement not only pays off in increased financial support for the institution but also pays off in the insights you gain that can help you do your development work better.

Experienced fundraisers also develop a list of reporters who are interested in the sorts of things that happen at the college or university and can be trusted to get the facts right. If a donor or an important member of the community is involved in the news item, representatives of the institution can serve as sources (where appropriate) so that the correct information is shared and (where necessary) another side of the story can be presented.

Making full use of the expert database mentioned earlier, a development office or public relations team can serve as a broker, bringing faculty members with a background relevant to a news story into contact with the journalists who are covering it. In certain cases, they can also provide access to the school's president, chair of the governing board, or another high-ranking administrator so that the media understands the institution's position on a topic or its processes in reaching a particular conclusion.

CASE STUDY

One day, you participate in a conference call with members of a fundraising initiative at another institution. They're looking for your help since you've gained a reputation as someone who knows how to make academic and development partnerships work. The problem the team is facing is that they're working in a community with a very strained town/gown relationship. Members of the community seem to care very little about the resource in their midst; they notice it only when campus events cause the traffic to become heavy or when a student from the school is arrested for underage drinking. Faculty members have little interaction with the local townspeople; many of them live in a residential community some distance away and pay attention to the local citizens only when they illegally park on campus.

"We don't know where to begin," a dean at the other school tells you during the call. "The programs that we're responsible for are almost unknown by people who live even a block or two from campus. The locals tend to feel that the only time they ever hear from us is when we're seeking donations. Virtually none of them have children who attend our school. Their feelings about us seem to run from indifferent to outright hostile, with very little of anything positive mixed in. We've tried offering the townspeople free tickets to campus events, but no one ever takes them. Frankly, we're out of ideas."

Question: What recommendations can you make to your colleagues?

Possible Strategies

The first thing you might suggest is that the group move from a passive to an active form of community engagement. In other words, instead of thinking of ways for the community to come to them, they might begin thinking of all the ways in which they can go to the community. Each member of the team can join one of the local service clubs. They can be highly visible at Chamber of Commerce events. They can volunteer to serve as speakers in local schools and at public events. They can meet people from the community where they tend to gather, such as in malls, at grocery stores, and outside movie theaters. They can initiate an annual recognition event for a distinguished member of the community, publicize that event through the local media, and send personal invitations to anyone who might be interested in attending.

It's not unusual for the communities in which colleges and universities are located to feel that they bear the brunt of the institution's fundraising efforts and that, as in the case study, "the only time they ever hear from you is when you're seeking donations." For this reason, you might want to encourage the development of an institution-wide policy that limits the types of solicitations made locally. Georgia Southern University, located in the small city of Statesboro, Georgia, tries to avoid this impression by holding an annual event that it calls "A Day for Southern": The idea is that the university will limit its solicitation of gifts from Statesboro residents to a single 24-hour period each year; that means that for every day local residents hear about the school's need for contributions, there will be 364 days in which they'll hear about the school's achievements and how it's giving back to the community. (See www. georgiasouthern.edu/a-day-for-southern/.)

You might also recommend that the development staff at the institution conduct a formal needs assessment of the community. Some towns are the most troubled by traffic problems. Others have difficulty attracting new businesses. Still others feel that their school system is inadequate. By identifying at least one clear need the community has, and then sincerely and very visibly addressing that need, the school can begin to mitigate some of the town/gown hostility that it's experiencing and to create a new style of interaction between themselves and local residents.

CONCLUDING THOUGHTS

To be candid, raising awareness can never be entirely separated from raising money. One of the main reasons why a college or university wants to foster good community relations is that it hopes to benefit from them: If a local community takes pride in the institution in its midst, it will send students, volunteers, and donations to that school. If a community feels cut off from or ignored by a college or university, it will tolerate its presence at best, and it will make its work much harder at worst. Community engagement arises because world-class fundraisers want to be good citizens—of their nation, their institution, and their community. But they also want to be good fundraisers. Raising positive awareness of their school in their community helps them achieve both these goals simultaneously.

REFERENCES

Buller, J. L. (2015). *Change leadership in higher education: A practical guide to academic transformation.* San Francisco, CA: Jossey-Bass.

Buller, J. L. (2016). *The essential academic dean or provost: A comprehensive desk reference.* (2nd Ed.) San Francisco, CA: Jossey-Bass.

RESOURCES

Crabill, S. L., & Butin, D. W. (2014). *Community engagement 2.0?: Dialogues on the future of the civic in the disrupted university.* New York, NY: Palgrave Macmillan.

Hoy, A. (2013). *Deepening community engagement in higher education: Forging new pathways.* New York, NY: Palgrave Macmillan.

Percy, S. L., Zimpher, N. L., & Brukardt, M. J. (2006). *Creating a new kind of university: Institutionalizing community-university engagement.* Bolton, MA: Anker.

Perkins, L. (2015). *The community manager's playbook: How to build brand awareness and customer engagement.* Berkeley, CA: Apress.

Watson, D. (2007). *Managing civic and community engagement.* Maidenhead, UK: Open University Press/McGraw-Hill.

Chapter Six

Listening to and Telling Stories

When people first become involved in development, they frequently know a great deal about what's in store: the need to be patient while cultivating prospective donors, the financial complexity of many gift agreements that will require extensive legal reviews, the importance of stewardship once a gift has been made, and so on. What they're often not expecting is just how important stories are to the fundraising process. Being a member of a world-class academic fundraising operation means that you're in the story-telling business. You routinely have an opportunity to tell others the story of what your institution does, why it's important, and how they might become a part of it. But even more important, you're in the business of listening to and analyzing stories, the stories that prospective donors tell you about their past successes and future goals. If you don't pay careful attention to these stories—perhaps because, instead of listening, you're thinking of the next thing you'll say—you can miss an opportunity to help your programs succeed and the prospect's dreams become reality.

TRULY LISTENING TO SOMEONE'S STORY

There's a huge difference between going through the motions of listening to a donor or prospect talk about past achievements and future priorities and truly listening to what they have to say, empathizing with their successes and frustrations, and finding areas where this person's needs and those of the institution overlap. Unsuccessful academic fundraisers are constantly wondering about how they can close the deal and get the money. World-class fundraisers take a more holistic approach. Naturally, they're eager to secure the funding that will allow the program to achieve an important goal. But they also view their donors as genuine stakeholders in their mission, not just as human piggy banks. They want to create a situation in which the donor is just as pleased about making the gift as the institution is about receiving it.

Listening to a story is, in its own way, as much a skill as telling a story. You have to be fully present, allowing the story to take you where the speaker wants to go, not merely looking for connections between what the donor's saying and where you want the story to go. Here are a few techniques you can use when listening to someone tell his or her story:

- *Watch the person's eyes, not his or her mouth.* It's often said that people's eyes "sparkle" or "light up" when they're favorably excited about something. See whether you can identify moments during the story when you see this phenomenon occur. A prospective donor may be talking about his success as a marketing representative for a Fortune 500 company but then make a passing reference to his granddaughter and entirely change his expression. That's an indication that it's this family connection, not the donor's career, that's his major source of joy these days. So, you may be speaking to this person because you were hoping for a gift to your marketing program, but that may not be his greatest passion now. Something that helps the donor's granddaughter (and others like her) may be a better philanthropic outlet for this person.
- *Don't interrupt, but offer oral and physical encouragement to the speaker.* If a potential donor is telling you about her success as a cardiologist, you can get the entire conversation offtrack if you interrupt with remarks like, "A cardiologist? Really? My cousin Chris was a cardiologist in the very town you were working in. Did you know Chris Johnson?" At the same time, you can derail the conversation by never moving or saying anything at all. An occasional nod (not so often that you look like a bobble-head doll), a softly spoken "Interesting," or a slight lean forward are all indications to the speaker that you're engaged in what he or she is saying and want to hear more.
- *Let the story tell itself.* In mindfulness training, such as the Mindfulness Based Stress Reduction program developed by Jon Kabat-Zinn at the University of Massachusetts Medical Center, the goal is to become non-judgmentally aware of each experience as it occurs. In other words, when our normally considerate friend Casey snaps at us one day, we often turn that experience into a story. "Why is Casey so mad at me? I wonder if he heard that I thought his treatment of that prospective donor last week was a bit abrupt. Of course, he's often so moody. Maybe he's got trouble at home. Or maybe . . . " By now, one curt remark has become the basis for an entire trilogy. Mindfulness encourages people to accept experiences for what they are and not force them to seem like something else. The same thing can

occur when we're listening to a story. We become tempted to hijack it and assume that it's going in the direction we expect it to. But stories often surprise us, and good listeners allow stories to proceed at their own pace and move in their own direction.

- *Visualize.* Stories are powerful because they paint pictures. But we can deprive them of their power if we don't allow the pictures they paint to emerge in our minds with all their lush details. As we'll see later, when we tell our own stories, we want prospective donors to put a face on a project: the successful scientist, the deserving student, or the talented playwright. We owe them the same courtesy. Visualizing what donors tell us allows us not merely to hear what they're saying but also to feel what they're feeling. And we're much more likely to reach a mutually satisfying conclusion as a result.
- *After the story, demonstrate appreciation.* Even if a prospective donor tells you the most boring story in the world—and even if you've heard it dozens of times earlier—he or she has done you a favor. The donor has granted you temporary access to the things that he or she finds exciting, disturbing, challenging, annoying, or awe-inspiring. When donors tell us their stories, we should feel privileged to have been admitted to a very personal corner of their world. So, after the story, thank them for their generosity. If the story was interesting and insightful, say so. If it wasn't, at least thank them for their courtesy in trusting you with such a personal account of their lives.

Once the prospective donor has shared his or her story (and even though we say *story*, it's not likely to be a single account but an entire series of stories told over many meetings), it's time to start looking for an overlap between whatever motivates the prospective donor and whatever best serves the needs of the institution. If the person is interested in giving back to the community, having his or her name commemorated, helping future generations, associating with people who are famous or brilliant, pursuing a lifelong passion, or achieving any other sort of goal, you're more likely to be in a better position to know how best to proceed now that you know what his or her story is. (For more on how to listen to stories, see Simmons, 2015, 177–186.)

CRAFTING AN EFFECTIVE STORY

When it's appropriate for a fundraiser to tell a story, it's important for that story to be well designed so as to be as effective as possible. But even though storytelling is such an integral part of what academic fundraisers do, it's given far too little attention in the criteria by which development officers (DOs) are certified or the programs by which they are trained. (For examples, of these criteria and programs, see Appendix II and Appendix III in the companion volume to this book, *World-Class Fundraising Isn't a Spectator Sport: The Team Approach to Academic Fundraising*, 2016.) Worse, as we'll see a bit later in this chapter, when training programs do provide guidance in how to tell stories, they sometimes focus on the wrong kinds of stories, at least as far as academic fundraising is concerned. Fortunately, there are abundant resources available on the art of effective storytelling. Since world-class fundraisers frequently get together with their colleagues to improve their skills, any one of these resources might provide the basis for a mini-retreat or an extended workshop. Among the best books available for providing concise and practical advice on how to craft an effective story are the following:

- Annette Simmons' *The Story Factor* (2009) describes why stories are usually more powerful than facts in persuading people to adopt or avoid a certain course of action. She also explains how to tell stories with your entire body (not by acting them out but through appropriate expressions and gestures) rather than with words alone.
- Simmons' *Whoever Tells the Best Story Wins* (2015) then applies these lessons to the rhetorical power of storytelling: using stories to advocate for a certain position or, as in the case of fundraising, attract people to a certain cause.
- Craig Wortmann's *What's Your Story?* (2012) provides specific advice about how to tell stories effectively, develop a story matrix (a catalog of suitable stories on various topics), and adapt storytelling to the needs of different professions, such as sales and management.
- Akash Karia's *TED Talks Storytelling* (2015) distills the lessons learned from the best presenters in the eighteen-minute format adopted by the popular Technology, Entertainment, and Design (TED) programs and develops them into a method that anyone can use to tell truly engaging stories.
- Cheryl Clarke's *Storytelling for Grantseekers* (2009), although it's primarily intended for those who wish to obtain funding from foundations, explores techniques that are equally useful when one is trying to make a cause come alive in the minds of individual donors.
- Dan Portnoy's *The Non-Profit Narrative* (2012) describes how fundraisers can use the familiar three-act structure common in plays, movies, and television programs to structure the stories they tell in a way that increases their impact.

All these guides to storytelling have their own preferred approaches and formal structures but, in general, the advice for crafting an effective fundraising narrative usually relies on six key principles.

1. *Get to the good stuff right away.* If you were writing a novel, a certain amount of exposition would be appropriate. You'd have to know a bit about each character's backstory in order to understand how he or she responds to the plot as it unfolds. But in the shorter, tighter form of storytelling required in advancement work, that amount of detail simply bogs the story down and causes the listeners to become less interested. Move immediately to the heart of the story and keep the plot simple.
2. *Focus on one or at most two central characters.* Even if you're talking about a discovery that was only possible through the work of a vast research team, concentrate on the principal investigator or a particularly interesting member of the team. For a fundraising story to be compelling, it needs a "face," someone whom the listener can identify with or feel inspired by. Stories without central characters aren't really stories at all; they're just bits of information tied together as though they were a story.
3. *Appeal to the senses.* Stories are more engaging when the listener can visualize what you're describing, and maybe even feel, smell, and taste it as well. Give your listeners a chance to imagine that they're actually witnessing the event instead of learning about it second hand. Immerse them in details that make the experience of the story more vivid.
4. *Place yourself in your listeners' position.* The people who are hearing the story are likely to have a different background from your own and that of the characters in the story. What might they not understand that will have to be explained? You don't want to talk down to your audience, but you don't want to leave them baffled either. You can include the explanatory material in passing, as in the following example, "And then Jane realized that she had no way to perform capnography, a way of measuring the amount of carbon dioxide the patient was exhaling. So, she came up with a very inventive solution . . . " Avoid talking in acronyms or abbreviations that your audience won't understand. If you're a classicist, the abbreviation APA means the American Philological Association. But if your listener is going to assume that the APA you're talking about is the American Psychological Association—perhaps because he or she learned the APA citation style in school—you're going to have a problem. When in doubt, spell it out. In addition, putting yourself in your audience's place means imagining the story from their perspective. What is the most likely to interest, concern, surprise, or delight them?
5. *Be yourself.* For some people, a conversational, folksy style seems perfect. For others, that style would appear as unnatural as it would if someone held the person at gunpoint and forced him to take off his Armani suit and put on overalls. Whether you realize it or not, you already have a storytelling style. It's the way you speak when you relate an interesting incident to a loved one or tell a friend what you enjoyed about your vacation. Aim

to adopt that voice, and your story will seem to flow naturally from who you are.

6. *Bring the story to a conclusion; don't just end it.* You're obviously telling this story for a reason. In many cases, that reason will be obvious to your audience. In other cases, they may not see the connection between the story and the rest of your conversation. So, you'll want to wind the story up by connecting it somehow to the present day or even the occasion where you are with your potential donors. "And that's why Paul decided to attend Fascinating Story State College instead of that other, more well-known university up the road. With your help, we can be sure that there will be a lot more Pauls in FSSC's future. Thank you very much."

Good storytelling falls somewhere between being an art and a science. Some people take to it more naturally than others, but everyone can become proficient at it. It simply takes practice, so that applying the Six principles listed earlier feels natural rather than formulaic. If you have regularly scheduled meetings that focus on development activities for your program, you have a built-in audience for practice runs of your story telling. Devote a few minutes at the end of a meeting to have each member of the team practice a new story on the other members. Learn from the techniques that work well for others but, as we saw earlier, remember to be yourself. If humor isn't your style, don't try to be humorous just because another member of your team is so good at telling funny stories. Getting better at telling stories isn't about adopting other people's style; it's about incorporating their best practices into your own unique style.

TELLING THE RIGHT STORY

Knowing how to shape and tell a story properly is, of course, an essential prerequisite for the effective use of narrative in fundraising. But it's also crucial to tell the right story. And it's in the choice of what kind of story to tell that many development workshops get it wrong, at least when it comes to the type of fundraising that occurs in higher education. Many people have classified stories in the past, breaking them down according to Jungian psychological theory, a universal taxonomy of folktale, and other (sometimes arcane) theoretical structures. For our purposes, we're simply interested in the types of story that fundraising professionals—and occasionally prospective donors—tell to describe what motivates them. From that perspective, we might break development stories into several key types.

- *Problem stories* are those in which a major challenge is posed, the solution to which has not yet been found. A story intended to urge the listener to contribute toward the curing of a disease or a severe social crisis is a problem story.
- *Adversity stories* are those in which the central character is demonstrated as overcoming a seemingly impossible obstacle, with the implication that others could be similarly successful if more funding were available. A story that describes a once-at-risk student who's now a thriving surgeon is an adversity story.
- *Self-sacrifice stories* are those that recount the selfless actions of a heroic individual, urging the hearer to help commemorate that person or eliminate the possibility that his or her sacrifice will be in vain. A story that tells of a graduate who traveled into a dangerous part of the world to alleviate suffering and died in the attempt is a self-sacrifice story.
- *Surprise stories* are those in which an assumption that had long been taken for granted is either questioned or disproven. A story that tells how students might graduate from college faster by taking fewer courses and doing less homework would be a surprise story.
- *Success stories* are those that describe an exciting achievement or a fascinating discovery, urging the listener to contribute to promote this important cause. A story that tells of a faculty member's breakthrough in determining the cause of a disease or that describes an author's award-winning play is a success story.
- *Vision stories* are those that present an attractive, almost utopian image of what the future could be and then encourages the hearer to help make that vision a reality. A story that imagines an entirely renovated campus with lower tuition rates and multiple endowed faculty positions is a vision story.

All six of these types of stories can be useful in academic fundraising. They are simply tools you can keep in your toolkit, pulling the right kind out for each specific situation. But here's the key point (and you'll notice that it's kind of a surprise story itself; see textbox 6.1):

Although much training in fundraising focuses on problem and adversity stories, the single most effective story in academic fundraising is a success story that becomes a vision story.

Let's unpack that statement to see why it's true. Problem and adversity stories are common in most types of fundraising, and it's easy to understand why. If you want to cure a disease, reduce poverty, eliminate a dangerous situation, or promulgate a religious doctrine, it's effective to make that challenge personal for the people hearing your story, to help them feel empathy for those who are suffering. Joseph Stalin probably never said, "The death of one man is a tragedy; the deaths of millions is a statistic." but, as cold-blooded as that sentiment is, there's a grain of truth in it. People frequently aren't moved to contribute toward the eradication of a disease that kills masses of people. But they frequently are moved when they hear the story of a single child who died of that illness.

In a similar way, people may not be willing to contribute to a cause that's responsible for distributing millions of free Bibles or Korans throughout the world, but they may be inclined to do so after hearing the story of a person whose life was utterly changed after receiving one of these free books. For this reason, when fundraising trainers work with deans, chairs, alumni directors, and DOs, they often encourage them to develop problem and adversity stories. "Tell us," they might say, "about a difficulty that you had to overcome in getting your college education. Make the audience feel the adversity you've faced." In one such program, the workshop leader tried repeatedly to get one university president to tell this kind of story, despite the president's strong resistance. "No one else is going to share their story," the presenter said, "unless you show that you're willing to share yours." Finally, in resignation to the inevitable, the president got up before the audience and said, "I myself grew up in what you might call straitened circumstances. At one of our winter homes, we had a few members of the domestic staff who didn't even have a college degree. If I hadn't been a legacy student, it's possible that my admission to Yale could have been somewhat harder." Needless to say, the story didn't have the effect that the trainer was expecting.

The fact is that people give to colleges, universities, and community colleges for different reasons than they give to other causes. They even give to higher education for different reasons than those that may have inspired them to contribute toward primary and secondary education. Contributors to early education are frequently concerned about access. They want to be sure that everyone in society has at least a certain minimum level of opportunity. And they're concerned about adversity; the at-risk student who overcomes obstacles to make an important social contribution is inspiring to them. But once the focus is on higher education, most people's concern switches from access to success. They want to be part of a winning team (sometimes literally in the case of contributions to athletic programs). They want to jump on the bandwagon of those talented researchers who cured (or are likely to cure) a terrible disease of feel part of remarkable piano program that's producing undergraduates who then go on to graduate studies at Juilliard. For higher education fundraising, the enticement of an optimistic vision is far more

I don't know how many of you know Dave Rudolph. Dave's one of those guys who'd never feel comfortable attending an event like this or talking about himself. You know the type: Always working late hours in the lab; always tinkering on something; always explaining it to you in ways that make you realize this is someone whose intelligence goes far beyond anything you can even imagine. Anyway, he's got this new undergraduate student working in his lab this year: Gina Meyer, bright as can be; she's going to *be* the next Dave someday.

The problem is that, because of a childhood illness, Gina has lost both legs from just above the knee. She's been getting around really well in a wheelchair, but it was sometimes a problem in the lab. She had to work at a specially lowered bench. She couldn't get around everywhere she wanted to be. She really needed a set of prosthetics that could give her the mobility that all of Dave's other lab workers had. Dave, being the kind of guy he is, looked into it for her. He was even going to pay for it. But to get the kind that Gina needed … well, the cost was just going to be too much.

So, one day in the lab, Dave turned to Gina and said, "Why don't we just build them ourselves?" At first, Gina thought this was kind of a crazy idea because the kind she needed were very complex in design. That's why they cost so much. But then she started thinking, "We've got the computer power here. We've got 3D printers. We've got all the talented design people we could ever need. Why not?" So, they set out to see if they could tackle the problem and—no exaggeration here—in less than two weeks they built a set of prosthetics that articulate completely and gave Gina as much mobility as you and I have. Probably more!

SUCCESS

Figure 6.1 Blended Story.

compelling than the threat of a pessimistic vision. And so, although academic fundraisers need to be able to tell all six types of stories—and keep ready examples in their repertoires for when they're needed—their virtuoso pieces should be success stories that become vision stories.

Here's an example of how that type of blended story works (See Figures 6.1 and 6.2.).

Notice how the person telling this story doesn't turn Gina's narrative into an adversity story or a self-sacrifice story (even though the basic plot could lend itself to either form). Instead, the focus remains positive throughout the story in order to build energy toward the excitement of the proposed vision in the second half. If the cause that was seeking donations had been a hospital or social service agency, those other types of stories—which play on the listener's sympathy and desire to alleviate suffering—tend to be effective. But for academic fundraising, the motivation of donors is more likely to be a desire to become part of an exciting new project or build on established successes. For that reason, the storyteller crafts the story in such a way that it meets the listeners' expectations and aligns with their philanthropic focus.

Gina, do you want to come up here and join me? *[From the audience, a young student
strides confidently up to the speaker. The speaker waits through a round of spontaneous
applause.]* Not even two days later, Dave drops by to see me. "Why can't we do for lots of
other people what we just did for Gina?" he asks. And he outlines a plan to develop all
kinds of prosthetic devices for people who don't have insurance and simply can't afford the
equipment they need. He's thinking big: Maybe help five hundred to a thousand people —
people right here in our community—every year. He wants to give hope to some folks who
... well, haven't had much to hope for lately. And the more he talks, the more excited he's
getting. And I'm getting excited just listening to him.

Now this is no small venture we're talking about. It's going to cost the university about
thirty-five million dollars just to gear up for it and maybe two to three million dollars every
year to run the project. But this would be a way for the university to give back to a
community that's given it so much. Of course, if I had my way, I'd call this the Dave
Rudolph Center for Innovative Prosthetics. But Dave won't hear of that. He says ideas are
cheap, and he's got a lot of them. So, he wants the naming rights to go to the person or
foundation that can fund at least twenty-five of the thirty-five million dollars it'll cost to get
the center going. And that center could have *your* name on it.

You see, Dave and Gina—they've already done the hard part. All that remains is for you to
see it in your heart to make this beautiful dream a reality.

VISION

Figure 6.2   Blended Story.

SELECTING THE PROPER SUBJECT

In most cases, the subject of your success and vision story will be dictated
by the object of your fundraising. In our earlier hypothetical example, the
subject of the story arose naturally from the desire to fund the new Center
for Innovative Prosthetics. But in certain cases, your plans may not be
focused to that degree of precision. For instance, a capital or endowment
campaign often consists of an attempt to fund specific projects (which,
thus, may suggest the topic of the story you want to tell) and the general
needs of the institution (which don't provide you with an easily identifiable "hook" for your story). In the latter case, you may need to engage in
additional creative brainstorming in order to identify a suitable subject for
a compelling story.

A good place to begin is with what Chip and Dan Heath call *bright
spots*: those things that are already working well. (See Heath and Heath,
2005.) The identification of bright spots is a key component in the practice
known as *appreciative inquiry* in which the goal is to find the strengths of
an organization and build on them (as opposed to the common management
practice of focusing on weaknesses and trying to eliminate them). But the
Heaths' bright spot concept is also an effective way of selecting the proper
subject of a story to tell when there is no immediately obvious subject. We
call the process that world-class fundraisers use to find a story worth telling
the *Screened Brainstorming Method*. Here's how it works.

At a meeting of academic and development personnel who are involved in a specific fundraising project, the group begins with a traditional brainstorming activity based on the questions, "What are our bright spots? What do we do better than anyone else? What are our positive distinctions?" As always with brainstorming, the first phase consists merely of listing ideas without judging them. You continue this process until people run out of ideas, but (and this is important) the group has to generate a list of at least eight ideas. Then once the list has been developed, the second phase of the process— the *screening* component of the Screened Brainstorming Method—is to go through the list and cross out any item that states or paraphrases any of the following ideas:

• Our faculty is excellent (superb, accomplished, distinguished).
• We care about our students.
• We keep our class sizes small.
• We're student oriented.
• We have an excellent (superb, distinctive) curriculum.
• We accomplish a great deal even though our funding is inadequate (or "We do a lot with a little.").
• Our graduates go on to accomplish great things.

The reason why you have to cross out these items is that they're the things that every college, university, and program believes about itself. That's right: Even though you can probably think of more than a dozen institutions whose budgets fill you with envy, the faculty and staff at those schools still see themselves as underfunded. You can probably think of plenty of schools where class sizes are far greater than yours and the quality of instruction strikes you as low; the people there still believe that they're keeping class sizes to a minimum and doing a terrific job with a marvelous curriculum. You now probably realize why your list of bright spots had to consist of at least eight items: The screening phase of the exercise could have caused you to eliminate as many as seven items from your list. If you started with fewer than eight entries, that kind of screening might leave you with no list at all. (For a similar exercise, see Buller, 2015, 60.)

The third phase of the Screened Brainstorming Method is to go through the items that now remain on your list and put them in order in three different ways: from most to least exciting; from most to least distinctive; and from most to least potentially appealing to donors. Look at the top one or two items on each list. If your experience is similar to ours every time we've done this exercise, the same item probably appears as number 1 on all three lists, or as number 1 on two lists, and numbers 2 or 3 on the other list. That's the proper subject for your story. It's a bright spot. It's exciting. It's distinctive. And it's likely to appeal to donors. Now just find a central character or two to serve as the "face" of that story, and get your creative juices flowing.

TELLING YOUR STORY INTERNALLY

In *The Department Chair Primer*, Don Chu (2012, 17–19) makes an important distinction between viewing a program or institution as a closed system (where one thinks of only the faculty, students, and administration) and viewing it as an open system (where one thinks of all the many stakeholders whom, both within and outside the school, the unit serves). Most of the time, this distinction becomes important when members of a development office have to broaden the view of faculty members and administrators who may think of their stakeholders as only being people inside the institution. But when it comes to their own perspective, academic fundraisers sometimes adopt the opposite perspective: They become so preoccupied with telling their story to external stakeholders that they may overlook the necessity of telling their story inside the institution as well. As a result, the program's internal constituents—the very people who should be its strongest supporters—feel left out of the loop, disengaged, and (at worst) treated as subordinates, not full partners, in the program's success.

World-class fundraisers understand that, as important as it is to be able to tell the institution's story to outsiders, it's also important for the faculty, staff, and students of the school to hear this story as well. In fact, there are three major types of stories that anyone involved in academic fundraising needs to share regularly with stakeholders within the college or university itself.

First, there's the *Behind the Scenes Story.* This type of story creates a type of camaraderie by conveying the message "we're all in this together." It's presented with a tone of "I wouldn't tell this to just anyone, but since we're all family here . . . " The story then proceeds to give the audience a behind-the-scenes glimpse into what current hopes and plans are for various development projects.

This type of story is particularly powerful with faculty members. Professors often feel a sense of power or authority that extends beyond their actual responsibilities. If something blindsides them, they complain that they should've been consulted or at least informed before such a major commitment was made. They feel very proprietary about any matter that affects the curriculum or that they believe is related to academic freedom or the standards they use to evaluate academic work.

For example, suppose that a donor endows a new faculty line in journalism. If the first time the faculty in that program hears about this gift is when it has been received, there's likely to be a surprising amount of pushback because the faculty had no role in helping to define the specialty of the new faculty position, how it will fit into the discipline's current plans, or whether the focus of the new position would overlap the responsibilities of a current member of the department.

Naturally, you don't want to give away sensitive details of a plan in advance; certain donors may become skittish if there's a public announcement that they're being cultivated. But a more general story about the sort of projects you're currently trying to fund—particularly if it includes an invitation to internal stakeholders to voice their opinion about how those projects should unfold—is extremely valuable. Faculty members know that their advice won't always be taken, but they do expect to have their perspectives heard.

The second major type of story that academic fundraisers need to share with their internal constituents is the *Why We're Excited Story.* The academic and development sides of an institution have distinctly different annual rhythms. For faculty members and academic administrators, the world is clearly divided by academic years. The year begins with the fall semester, enters a lull during winter break, recovers a bit of its energy with the spring semester, and goes on hiatus during the summer. That pattern means that optimism and energy are at their highest each August and September, and at their lowest in April and May, a time when frustrations and tempers may rise.

The development side of the institution is certainly aware of those rhythms, but it's less governed by them than are colleges and academic departments. For DOs, there may be a sense that one year is ending and a new one is beginning each June and July (when most institutions have the start of a new fiscal calendar), combined with a similar sense that one year is ending and a new one is beginning each December and January (when contributions tend to be timed so that they fall in one tax year or another). But even these two patterns are less ingrained in the lives of people than is the academic year for faculty members and academic administrators.

For this reason, DOs sometimes have to be sensitive to the fact that some of their internal stakeholders may respond to initiatives in ways that may initially seem puzzling. An idea that was embraced in late August can meet strong opposition in late March.

The Why We're Excited Story is an effort to counterbalance this tendency. It's an upbeat narrative that simultaneously flatters the audience and presents them with an optimistic vision of the future. At its simplest, its structure may be defined as "since you're so wonderful, we're now able to do even greater things." If a Why We're Excited Story is told simply to manipulate listeners, it's unlikely to have an effect that's significant or lasting.

In order to be effective, the storyteller has to identify a set of reasons why he or she truly admirers the stakeholders and connect those reasons in a plausible manner to the cause that's being proposed. It might unfold as we see in the following example:

> One of the qualities for which the College of Ratiocination is so justly celebrated is the capacity you all have to link genuinely cutting-edge research with the needs of students at both the undergraduate and graduate level. I know I'm always impressed by the creativity with which you infuse your own independent scholarship into the curriculum so that your graduates go on to become successful in their lives and careers. Even on my worst days—and we all have them—the thing that brings me to work in the morning is knowing that the external funding we generate will help your students through scholarship, research travel, improved facilities, and other expenditures essential to their education. That's why I know I can count on you as we move into this capital campaign that's going to ratchet all of that up to the next level. Just imagine what it's going to be like when the College of Ratiocination has its own state-of-the-art facility right in the center of campus. Imagine what it'll be like when you'll be able to recruit ten or twelve of the best students anywhere who'll be able to attend your program tuition-free. Picture what it'll be like when you have funding to attend multiple international conferences each year, bringing your research team with you if you'd like, so that you can carry your program's story even further. That's why I know I can count on you to go with us as we make donor calls, meet with foundations, and do all the necessary background work we'll need to do to make those dreams a reality. I know you'll do it because you've already demonstrated a willingness to do even more difficult things if they'll build your program and help your students.

A good Why We're Excited Story should leave the audience feeling a share of that excitement and renewed with the type of energy they bring to their jobs after a summer break or an extended sabbatical.

The third important type of story that academic fundraisers use for internal consumption is the *Recognition and Appreciation Story*. We can think of this type of story as a form of internal stewardship. It celebrates the achievements of those who have worked to reach a certain goal, makes them feel that their efforts meant something important, and inspires others who want someday to receive that type of public attention. In order to be effective, a Recognition and Appreciation Story has to be specific. It can't say simply, "Thanks, everyone, for all you do. You're all wonderful." It has to talk about the specific contributions of specific people. As such, it poses several challenges that other types of stories may not have.

First, this type of story is the most effective when the people being recognized are present but unaware that the recognition is coming. For a very introverted person, like Dave Rudolph in our blended story earlier in this chapter, it's acceptable, even desirable, to bestow praise when the person isn't there to be embarrassed or (worse) angered by the attention. But otherwise, Recognition and Appreciation Stories tend to fall flat when members of the audience can't turn toward the person they're celebrating, break out with applause at the end, and then line up to offer the person their own congratulations. That effect is all the greater when the recognition comes as a surprise.

So, unless you're absolutely certain that the person will be in attendance anyway when the story is told, there may be a need for some mild deception that will cause the person to be present under false pretenses. Most people who are honored in this way have earned the recognition because they devoted time to caring for others. They can, thus, often be persuaded to attend the event by being told that the meeting is being held to honor someone else, and you know that he or she won't want to be left out of that opportunity.

The other challenge Recognition and Appreciation Stories pose is that, because they must focus on the achievements of a very select group of individuals, other people may feel left out. It's useful, therefore, to include language that you're recognizing someone as a representative of the work of many people and that others could just as easily have been chosen for this honor. Using your own words to express thoughts like the following can often be quite effective:

> Now you know that the administrative assistants in the college have all been invaluable for the success of this year's phonathon. When I heard stories of how every single one of them went far beyond the call of duty in making sure that our call lists were accurate, the student callers were well prepared to deal with every possible situation, the equipment was all set up and ready to go—why, it almost knocked me over. We don't have time to tell you all their stories—even though I wish I could; you'd be impressed, too—I do want to share a couple with you. Donna and Gavin, can you come up here for a second? I need to embarrass you for a few minutes by bragging about you. While they join me here, I want to make it clear that what these two did was typical of the kind of contribution everyone connected with this effort made. But maybe you'll understand how all of them made contributions that were truly remarkable if you hear just a few examples. Donna, let's start with you . . .

USING SOCIAL MEDIA EFFECTIVELY

Not all stories that a good fundraiser will tell are told in the presence of the audience. With the rise of social media, there are many new opportunities for academic officers (AOs), DOs, and any other member of the team to carry an institution's message to new audiences. But telling a story through social media requires following a different set of rules than you might use when telling a traditional story.

Since, as we saw in Chapter Five, new social media sites appear all the time (and yesterday's hot site becomes today's outdated fad), we won't consider guidelines that may apply to only particular sites. Rather, the things to keep in mind when telling a story by social media generally include the following:

- *Be concise.* Perhaps more than any other form of communication, social media requires brevity. You probably know this through your own experience: You come across a hyperlink to a news story that seems interesting or an item you might want to purchase; you click on the link, and it stops loading after a few seconds; you wait briefly—perhaps no more than ten or fifteen seconds total—before deciding it's not worth it and move on to something else. That's about how long you have to engage someone's interest in social media: ten to fifteen seconds. Even though you want to be concise in every story you tell—no one likes a storyteller who rambles on—brevity is essential to social media. Boil your story down to its key elements and tell only those.
- *Engage all the senses of the audience.* One reason why you can afford to be sparing with words in social media is that this form of communication doesn't depend on words alone. Depending on the form of social media you're using, you may be able to embed movies, background music, hyperlinks to other sites, sounds, and other forms of video and audio media.

Even if you're not able to convey tastes and fragrances directly through social media, you can invoke memories of them through well-chosen images. (One of the authors used to give a presentation in which the background slides all had a picture of a lavender field in the south of France. It was always surprising to see the number of evaluations that referred to the use of lavender perfume throughout the workshop, even though there wasn't any.)

- *Aim at the heart first, the brain only afterward.* Although social media sites are useful tools for conveying information, their real strength is in the conveying of emotions. Concise, well-chosen text, accompanied by moving images and sounds, can place the recipient into a properly receptive mood for whatever message you're trying to express. With alumni, that mood might include nostalgia for their time at the institution. With high-end donors, that mood might include awe at the cutting-edge technology in use at the school or the exotic locations at which students can study abroad.

In constructing a story for social media, ask yourself first, "What mood do I want the audience to be in so that this message will have its greatest impact?" By answering that question, you'll go a long way toward deciding exactly what you need to include in the message and what can be dismissed as extraneous.

- *Establish an identifiable tone or style.* Institutions have personalities just as people do. In all probability, your social media messages are going to appear to originate from a specific person (such as the president or a dean) or the institution as a whole.

What tone best conveys who that person or institution is? Is the president a warm and unpretentious sort of person who's comfortable speaking to almost anyone? Then perhaps aim at a conversational tone with plenty of contractions (e.g., *don't* for *do not*) and a few personal references ("Our daughter Julie was just telling us that . . . "). Is the institution relatively new or in the process of redefining itself? Then perhaps adopt a tone that's a bit more brash and filled with attitude. In general, try to develop a style that conveys who the speaker is and doesn't undermine the message by seeming flippant when it should be serious, formal when it should be casual, and so on.

- *Time your story to suit the audience.* If your message is intended for people with full-time jobs, having it appear over the weekend is a poor idea. By the time they get to their computers or tablets on Monday morning, dozens of other messages will have superseded it. If your message is intended for traditional-aged high school or college students, don't send it too early in the day. This age group frequently sleeps in and becomes more active in the afternoon or evening.

If your message is intended for an older group of donors, consider what platforms of social media they're likely to use and when. They may not be as up-to-date as students or current employees are, so you may need to broaden your message so that it appears through multiple platforms and reaches them in the late morning when they're more likely to be using their computers, smart phones, and tablets.

- *Make the story engaging enough that the reader will forward it to others.* The ultimate goal of any social media storyteller is for a message to "go viral": be frequently forwarded and reforwarded by successive groups of recipients. You certainly can't count on each message you post achieving a success rate like that, but you can increase the likelihood that a reader will forward it to someone else by making it amusing, surprising, inspiring, or touching.

Which of those you choose will depend on two factors we've already considered: the mood you want the recipient to be in and the tone or style of the message's author. As an example, a message announcing a social

126 *Chapter Six*

event for donors should be amusing and/or surprising, whereas a plea for funding to address a specific need is more likely to succeed if it's inspiring or touching.

- *If you're not comfortable with social media, work with someone who is.* Engaging in fundraising for an academic program or institution doesn't mean you have to do it all by yourself. If social media doesn't suit your interest or style, find someone who loves this form of communication. Even if you're the dean or a vice president for development and the other person is ghostwriting social media messages for you, you're far more likely to be successful by delegating this responsibility to someone who's good at it than by doing it merely because you think you're supposed to and producing stilted, awkward, or dull messages.

CASE STUDY

You're having a meeting to discuss various upcoming projects and fundraising activities. The goal of your meeting is to determine how best to use storytelling effectively for each project or activity, who should tell the story, and anything else that would make the story more effective.

For the purposes of this exercise, imagine those in attendance at your meeting are yourself, Jean Seligson (the vice president for student affairs), Ellen Crawford (an academic dean), Kwame Okafor (a department chair), Christine Chen (a DO), Bert Allen (the alumni director), Heather Wainwright (the athletic director), Tom McNab (a faculty member), and Maria Sanchez (the president of the student government association). When needed, Morgan Quinn, the school's president, also joins the group. (If one of these people happens to hold the title that you have, assume that, for whatever reason, there are two of you present at the meeting in related, but not overlapping positions. If you're the president, then assume that Morgan Quinn is the provost.)

Keep in mind that the point of the exercise isn't to develop a full story, which will probably be impossible in any case, but rather to decide how best to use storytelling in this situation, who should tell the story, and other related matters.

A. Recent tuition increases have meant that, during the past few years, a number of good students have had to drop out before graduating. The decision has been made to start an annual golf tournament and to use the proceeds to fund a number of need-based scholarships.
B. Tom McNab, the faculty member on the team, recently published a best-selling novel about a professor who works for a secret government

agency. The team hopes that by hosting an event in Tom's honor, it can help raise some research and travel funds for the English Department.

C. Dale Davenport, a local businessman who runs a highly successful chain of health clubs, is being cultivated as a possible donor to endow a new faculty position. He'll be having lunch with several members of the team next week, and the group needs to decide who should attend.

D. Alumni giving has been on a downward trend for several years. Despite efforts to find the reason, there doesn't appear to be any easily identifiable cause. The team wants to find a way to reverse this trend.

E. The institution's capital campaign has been going reasonably well, but it looks as though it may need one last big push to put the amount raised safely over the published goal.

Question: What recommendations do you make to your colleagues regarding each situation?

Possible Strategies

Although it may be unusual for any institution to be facing all five of these situations simultaneously, it's not at all unusual for situations similar to these to arise at a college or university. Since the focus of this unit is on storytelling, you might consider recommending the following strategies for each of the preceding situations:

A. This set of circumstances is probably the best addressed by having the vice president for student affairs and the president of the student government association make remarks during an appropriate moment at the tournament. Jean Seligson could begin by setting the stage. She could outline some of the reasons why tuition increases were inevitable and perhaps tell the story of one or two students who were the most severely affected by the cost increase.

Although, as we saw, academic fundraising is usually the best served by a success story that turns into a vision story, Seligson probably should deliver her remarks in the form of an adversity story in order to underscore the severity of the problem. She would then introduce Maria Sanchez, who could provide the student perspective.

A good strategy might be to continue the student stories begun by Seligson, particularly if one had a happy ending (a scholarship from a generous donor allowed the student to remain at the school) and one had an unhappy ending (the other student is currently working full time and, though there's hope that this student may return to the school, nothing is definite at this time).

If it happens to be that Sanchez herself was the student who was able to stay because of the scholarship, the result would be an adversity story that changed into a surprise story as well as a vision story (because those in attendance now have a clear understanding of how their gifts can help individual students).

B. It's clear that, in this case, Tom McNab himself should tell the story unless he happens to be particularly unsuited for this role. The precise nature of the story he tells is probably less important than the tone it conveys. For example, he could talk about how the idea for the novel came to him, similarities to and (perhaps humorous) differences between him and the professor in the novel. Whatever the subject, the story should leave the audience impressed by the quality of the school's faculty and fortunate to have such a successful author among its ranks.

C. The attendees at this lunch should definitely include the dean (as the highest ranking AO on the team), the DO, and either the faculty member or, if Dale Davenport is a significant enough prospect, the president.

Since the purpose is to endow a faculty position, what's probably needed is a success story that becomes a vision story that is closely related to the discipline of the position being sought. In any case, the goal should be to leave Davenport impressed by the work of the institution and, if possible, filled with FOMO (the Fear Of Missing Out on an important opportunity).

D. Since the goal is to get alumni giving back on track, a useful strategy is to strike a chord of nostalgia with graduates and enthusiasm about the institution's current direction. If most alumni are relatively young and technologically proficient, this situation would be a good opportunity to engage in some social marketing storytelling, perhaps with words of greeting from popular professors and a button that readers could use to make an immediate contribution. If most alumni are older and unlikely to use social media, a letter of no more than one page from the president or another senior administrator with a touching and nostalgic tone could be very effective.

E. Bringing the capital campaign to a successful conclusion might call for a combined effort of the president and athletic director to restore a new level of excitement to the campaign and bring the effort to a close. Vision stories that are rich in FOMO will be the most likely to bring about the desired level of success.

CONCLUDING THOUGHTS

A surprising amount of development work involves stories. World-class academic fundraisers listen to the stories of potential donors and try to match their philanthropic interests with the needs of the institution. They also need to be able to tell their institution's story in a way that's interesting, compelling, and memorable. Most frequently, these stories will be told in person, possibly at meetings with a donor and possibly at public events. For this reason, fundraisers need to be comfortable telling a wide range of stories in different settings using different media.

Although storytelling is too important a development activity to be assigned merely to one person, it's not necessary for everyone involved in a fundraising project to be a master of all the types and forms of stories discussed in this chapter. Different people will have different strengths, and it's better to assign people responsibilities based on their strengths than to assume that there's only a single profile for everyone involved in academic fundraising.

In Chapter 4, we saw that the last line of Aristotle's *Nicomachean Ethics* is, "Now let's begin," suggesting that once one had explored what one needed to do as an individual (ethics), it was time to begin exploring what one needed to do as a member of a group (politics). In much the same way, this book has been an examination of what individual members of the faculty, staff, or administration need to know in order to "go for the gold" and become world-class fundraisers.

The next step is to move from developing your own skills to developing a team of people with complementary skills who can help take your success in fundraising to the next level. For that reason, this book has a companion volume, *World-Class Fundraising Isn't a Spectator Sport: The Team Approach to Academic Fundraising* (2016). In it, you'll discover ways of putting the concepts covered in this book to work with even bigger projects that are capable of bringing you even more amazing results. A *team approach* means that members can play to their strengths, and help each other succeed in even the most challenging fundraising environments.

With that thought in mind, now let's begin.

REFERENCES

Buller, J. L. (2015). *The essential academic dean or provost: A comprehensive desk reference*. San Francisco, CA: Jossey-Bass.

Buller, J. L., & Reeves, D. M. (2016). *World-class fundraising isn't a spectator sport: The team approach to academic fundraising*. Lanham, MD: Rowman and Littlefield.

Chu, D. (2012). *The department chair primer: Leading and managing academic departments*. (2nd Ed.) San Francisco, CA: Jossey-Bass.

Clarke, C. A. (2009). *Storytelling for grantseekers: A guide to creative nonprofit fundraising*. (2nd Ed.) San Francisco, CA: Jossey-Bass.

Heath, C., & Heath, D. (2005). *Switch: How to change things when change is hard.* New York, NY: Broadway Books.

Karia, A. (2015). *TED Talks storytelling: 23 storytelling techniques from the best TED talks.* North Charleston, SC: CreateSpace.

Portnoy, D. (2012). *The non-profit narrative: How telling stories can change the world.* Pasadena, CA.: Portnoy Media Group.

Simmons, A. (2009). *The story factor: Secrets of influence from the art of storytelling.* (2nd Ed.) New York, NY: Basic Books.

Simmons, A. (2015). *Whoever tells the best story wins: How to use your own stories to communicate with power and impact.* (2nd Ed.) New York, NY: AMACOM.

Wortmann, C. (2012). *What's your story?: Using stories to ignite performance and be more successful.* (2nd Ed.) Evanston, IL: Sales Engine.

RESOURCES

Kawasaki, G., & Fitzpatrick, P. (2014). *The art of social media: Power tips for power users.* New York, NY: Portfolio.

Mead, G. (2014). *Telling the story: The heart and soul of successful leadership.* San Francisco, CA: Jossey-Bass.

Walter, E., & Gioglio, J. (2014). *The power of visual storytelling: How to use visuals, videos, and social media to market your brand.* New York, NY: McGraw-Hill.

Appendix A

Finding, Hiring, and Evaluating a Development Officer

Although successful groups of academic fundraisers treat one another as complete equals and respect the skills that each of their colleagues brings to the task, there's one area in which an academic officer (AO) and a development officer (DO) tend to differ: Although a DO rarely, if ever, is responsible for finding, hiring, and evaluating an AO, an AO may often be called on to select and evaluate a DO. For this reason, this appendix is designed to help academic administrators understand what to look for when choosing DOs for their areas.

FINDING THE RIGHT DEVELOPMENT OFFICER

Academic administrators tend to be very comfortable reading a faculty member's *curriculum vitae* because they know what to look for and what constitutes appropriate training. They may also be comfortable serving on a search committee for another administrator. But what training should a fundraiser have? Does the person have to have an actual degree in development? If someone is experienced in fundraising for, say, a hospital, is that background adequate preparation for development in higher education?

In order to answer these questions, it's important to recognize that academic administrators and DOs usually come to their positions by very different paths. The administrator will often have easily verifiable credentials: an advanced degree, prior leadership experience, experience in managing programs, rankings and evaluations by supervisors, peers, and direct reports, and so on. DOs, however, are members of a relatively new profession that attracts people from many different backgrounds. Academic programs and degrees in fundraising are just now coming of age. As a result, most DOs who have been involved with fundraising for fifteen years or more tend to have started out in another field and moved into fundraising mid-career. It's, thus, not at all uncommon for the DO to receive professional training only while on the job. There are several excellent programs—such as the Indiana University's Center on Philanthropy, New York University's George H. Heyman, Jr. Center for Philanthropy and Fundraising, and the Stanford Center for Philanthropy and Civil Society—that serve as valuable resources on everything related to philanthropy and fundraising. In addition, certain universities provide certificates or degrees in fundraising and/or nonprofit management. (See Appendix II of *World-Class Fundraising Isn't a Spectator Sport: The Team Approach to Academic Fundraising* for a list of some representative programs.)

One credential that many DOs seek is Certified Fund Raising Executive (CFRE) certification, a distinction earned after working in fundraising for a minimum of five years and passing an examination that covers the following areas:

- Prospect identification
- Solicitation
- Donor relations
- Volunteerism
- Management
- Stewardship

The content involved in CFRE certification appears in Appendix III of *World-Class Fundraising Isn't a Spectator Sport: The Team Approach to Academic Fundraising*. An advanced certificate (ACFRE) is also available, and renewal of the CFRE requires continuing education in the field.

A more recent addition to credentialing for fundraisers is the Chartered Advisory in Philanthropy (CAP) certification, offered by the American College of Financial Services. This designation requires successful completion of three graduate-level courses. Students complete the program through self-study and then take an examination at a local center. (See theamerican-college.edu/financial-planning/cap-philanthropy.) In the United Kingdom, the Institute of Fundraising offers several types of credentials, such as a Certificate in Fundraising, a Diploma in Fundraising, and a Certificate in Direct Marketing. (See institute-of-fundraising.org.uk/events-and-training/qualifications/.)

DOs function as "bridge" professionals in the sense that they represent both the organization to prospective donors and prospective donors to the organization. Even though their loyalty remains, of course, with the college or university employing them, DOs sometimes must serve as the donor's advocate, reminding the institution of the benefactor's intent and seeing that all commitments are honored. At the same time, a DO needs to be transparent when explaining university policies and restrictions to the donor, sometimes pointing out that what the person wants to accomplish isn't possible or can't become a priority for the institution. For this reason, DOs sometimes feel as though they're continually translating the vocabulary of higher education to prospective donors and the wishes of perspective donors to the college or university.

WHAT DOES A DEVELOPMENT OFFICER DO?

In order to advertise for the right DO, academic administrators need to think through what a DO actually does and, more specifically, what he or she will do in the academic area associated with the position. Job descriptions for DOs can vary widely. In general, however, there are eight important components to keep in mind when constructing a job description or position announcement for a DO.

1. The precise title that the person will hold
2. The qualifications or experience required for the position
3. His or her line of report. In other words, who will supervise and evaluate this person?
4. The units of the institution with whom the person will work
5. The types of fundraising for which the person will be responsible
6. Any other specific duties that are assigned to the officer
7. Skills that the officer must have
8. Required, preferred, or desired qualities, qualifications, and attributes

Here is how these eight components might appear in an advertisement developed by a hypothetical university:

Northwest Central Southern University is seeking a director of development for its College of Academic Jargon. The director will report jointly to the dean of the college and the vice president of advancement, and will be assigned an office in the Limited Resources Academic Building. The director will be responsible for identifying, cultivating, soliciting, and stewarding a portfolio of prospects that may include friends, parents, and alumni of the college, as well as other duties as assigned. The successful applicant will collaborate with the dean in developing and executing fundraising strategies for effective cultivation, be responsible for engaging donors in college events, strengthen relationships with prospects and donors, and promote university-wide campaigns on a regular basis. The director will work with faculty and staff to develop and implement cultivation and solicitation strategies, with primary emphasis on gifts of $50,000 or more from individuals, foundations, and corporations. Required qualifications include a bachelor's degree (advanced degree preferred) and a minimum of five years of progressively responsible fundraising experience, with documentation of success in raising at least one gift larger than $100,000. The successful candidate must:

✓ demonstrate commitment to the highest standards of personal and professional integrity and adhere to the best practices of fundraising.
✓ have exceptionally strong skills in verbal and written communication and in developing interpersonal relationships.
✓ be a team player and yet be able to work independently with little direct supervision.
✓ think creatively about potential new methods to achieve goals.
✓ exhibit the skills that are needed to operate effectively in high-level social and business situations.
✓ understand the importance of confidentiality and discretion with prospect and/or donor information.

Preference may be given to candidates with capital campaign experience and the ability to work with commonly used software applications in word processing, database management, and fundraising management.

There are several important elements that we can identify in this advertisement that tell us what type of DO this particular school is looking for.

• The university is looking for an experienced, mid-level professional. The title of the person will be director (as opposed to associate director or simply DO), the successful applicant will be expected to work independently, and the gifts that are specifically mentioned fall within the middle range of most institution's goals ($50,000–$100,000), although capital campaign experience is cited as desirable.
• The DO is going to have a divided reporting relationship. Though not uncommon in advancement, these divided lines of report always merit some investigation by the applicant before accepting the position. For instance, in our hypothetical advertisement, the director's office is in an academic building and thus possibly not with the rest of the advancement staff in an administration building. It will be unclear from this job description whether the DO reports primarily to the dean of Academic Jargon, with the vice president for advancement taking only a secondary role, or whether some other configuration is implied. It is also not readily apparent whether the dean and vice president clearly understand which of them will be in charge of which aspect of the person's responsibilities. For example, in a case of divided loyalties, will the director know which side he or she

should be on? When interviewing candidates, the AO or other members of the search committee will need to clarify these issues.

- The word *preferred* is used with regard to an advanced degree, capital campaign experience, and familiarity with common software applications. The person or committee in charge of hiring the successful applicant will need to have given sufficient thought to how that term is being used in this context. Does it mean that if any applicant has one or more of these qualifications, he or she is automatically given preference to the other candidates? Or does it mean only that, if it comes down to a final choice between two otherwise comparable applicants, the one with the most of these qualifications may have a slight edge? Different institutions approach preferred qualifications in different ways. Before inviting candidates to interview for this position, the AO or search committee will need to decide how it will treat preferred qualifications with regard to semifinalists and finalists for the position. Otherwise, one person is likely to review credentials in one way whereas others review them quite differently.

- Although the advertisement initially appears to detail the responsibilities of the position quite precisely, it also includes the phrase *other duties as assigned*. Depending on the institution, that phrase could mean practically anything. Some DOs discover only on taking the position that these "other duties" occupy far more of their time than do the responsibilities outlined in their position description. So, the dean and vice president will need to have a clear picture of how much latitude will be given to these additional duties before selecting the successful candidate. Having that information clearly in mind will help those who are interviewing candidates identify relevant skills and be able to respond more authoritatively to questions from applicants.

The job description you write for a position will differ from our hypothetical example depending on how the eight components of a DO position are configured at your own institution. Once the advertisement is done, try looking at it from the perspective of someone working full-time in development. Even better, have a current DO review your text and see what assumptions he or she makes about the position and what questions arise.

Common questions you can expect from applicants are as follows:

- Why is this position available now?
- If it is a new position, what need led to its creation?
- If someone previously held the position, why did he or she leave it?
- If someone previously held the position, what were his or her strengths and areas of weaknesses?

• What would make the successful candidate's supervisor(s) declare that the person was successful after the first year on the job?

EVALUATION OF DEVELOPMENT OFFICERS

Once the academic administrator has hired a DO, there will need to be some way of determining whether the new fundraiser is doing a good job. Should the decision be based simply on the amount of money raised? Does effort count, even if it doesn't result in an actual gift? How should the supervisor account for the fact that gifts are somewhat unpredictable? After all, a terrific year may be followed by several poor ones. Does that mean that the DO did a good job in the successful year but not afterward? To begin with, it's important to recognize that DOs are evaluated on much more than the bottom line alone. Certainly, the amount raised by the DO is important, but so are such metrics as the following:

• The number of visits made to individual donors and prospects per year (150 is a common benchmark)
• The number of proposals submitted to individuals or foundations (i.e., the number of cultivation efforts that led to a specific ask)
• The number of new prospects added to the database each year
• Community engagement "contact points," such as membership in civic organization, attendance at events as a representative of the institution, and activity with community advisory boards
• The rate at which the funds that have been raised are increasing or decreasing from year to year

All DOs are expected to adhere to the Association of Fundraising Professionals (AFP) Code of Ethical Principles and Standards of Professional Practice (Appendix II) and the Donor Bill of Rights (Appendix III). The Donor Bill of Rights specifies what contributors can expect from fundraisers and the organizations that benefit from their philanthropy. This code supports transparency in explaining all relevant policies and indicates that organizations are accountable for reporting how they use the funds that they've received. Moreover, the AFP Code of Ethical Principles and Standards of Professional Practice provide guidelines on how DOs should be remunerated and how they should conduct themselves in accordance with the highest ethical standards.

Appendix B

AFP Code of Ethical Principles and Standards of Professional Practice

Association of Fundraising Professionals
Code of Ethical Standards (adopted 1964; amended 2014)[1]

The Association of Fundraising Professionals (AFP) believes that ethical behavior: (1) fosters the development and growth of fundraising professionals and the fundraising profession; and (2) enhances philanthropy and volunteerism. AFP members recognize their responsibility to ethically generate—or support the ethical generation of—philanthropic support. Violation of the standards may subject the members to disciplinary sanctions as provided in the AFP Ethics Enforcement Procedures. AFP members, both individual and business, agree to abide (and to ensure, to the best of their ability, that all members of their staff abide) by the AFP standards.

PUBLIC TRUST, TRANSPARENCY, AND CONFLICTS OF INTEREST

Members shall:

1. not engage in activities that harm the members' organizations, clients, or profession or knowingly bring the profession into disrepute.
2. not engage in activities that conflict with their fiduciary, ethical, and legal obligations to their organizations, clients, or profession.
3. effectively disclose all potential and actual conflicts of interest; such disclosure does not preclude or imply ethical impropriety.
4. not exploit any relationship with a donor, prospect, volunteer, client, or employee for the benefit of the members or the members' organizations.

5. comply with all applicable local, state, provincial, and federal civil and criminal laws.
6. recognize their individual boundaries of professional competence.
7. present and supply products and/or services honestly and without misrepresentation.
8. establish the nature and purpose of any contractual relationship at the outset and be responsive and available to parties before, during, and after any sale of materials and/or services.
9. never knowingly infringe the intellectual property rights of other parties.
10. protect the confidentiality of all privileged information related to the provider/client relationships.
11. never disparage competitors untruthfully.

SOLICITATION AND STEWARDSHIP OF PHILANTHROPIC FUNDS

Members shall:

12. ensure that all solicitation and communication materials are accurate and correctly reflect their organizations' mission and use of solicited funds.
13. ensure that donors receive informed, accurate, and ethical advice about the value and tax implications of contributions.
14. ensure that contributions are used in accordance with donors' intentions.
15. ensure proper stewardship of all revenue sources, including timely reports on the use and management of such funds.
16. obtain explicit consent by donors before altering the conditions of financial transactions.

TREATMENT OF CONFIDENTIAL AND PROPRIETARY INFORMATION

Members shall:

17. not disclose privileged or confidential information to unauthorized parties.
18. adhere to the principle that all donor and prospect information created by, or on behalf of, an organization or a client is the property of that organization or client.
19. give donors and clients the opportunity to have their names removed from lists that are sold to, rented to, or exchanged with other organizations.

20. when stating fundraising results, use accurate and consistent accounting methods that conform to the appropriate guidelines adopted by the appropriate authority.

COMPENSATION, BONUSES, AND FINDER'S FEES

Members shall:

21. not accept compensation or enter into a contract that is based on a percentage of contributions; nor shall members accept finder's fees or contingent fees.
22. be permitted to accept performance-based compensation, such as bonuses, only if such bonuses are in accord with prevailing practices within the members' own organizations and are not based on a percentage of contributions.
23. neither offer nor accept payments or special considerations for the purpose of influencing the selection of products or services.
24. not pay finder's fees, commissions, or percentage compensation based on contributions.
25. meet the legal requirements for the disbursement of funds if they receive funds on behalf of a donor or client.

NOTE

1. © 1964, Association of Fundraising Professionals (AFP), all rights reserved. Reprinted with permission from the Association of Fundraising Professionals.

Appendix C

Donor Bill of Rights

The Donor Bill of Rights was created by the Association of Fundraising Professionals (AFP), the Association for Healthcare Philanthropy (AHP), the Council for Advancement and Support of Education (CASE), and the Giving Institute: Leading Consultants to Non-Profits. It has been endorsed by numerous organizations.

THE DONOR BILL OF RIGHTS[1]

Philanthropy is based on voluntary action for the common good. It is a tradition of giving and sharing that is primary to the quality of life. To ensure that philanthropy merits the respect and trust of the general public, and that donors and prospective donors can have full confidence in the nonprofit organizations and causes they are asked to support, we declare that all donors have the following rights:

I. To be informed of the organization's mission, of the way the organization intends to use donated resources, and of its capacity to use donations effectively for their intended purposes

II. To be informed of the identity of those serving on the organization's governing board, and to expect the board to exercise prudent judgment in its stewardship responsibilities

III. To have access to the organization's most recent financial statements

IV. To be assured that their gifts will be used for the purposes for which they were given

V. To receive appropriate acknowledgement and recognition

VI. To be assured that information about their donation is handled with respect and confidentiality to the extent provided by law

VII. To expect that all relationships with individuals representing organizations of interest to the donor will be professional in nature

VIII. To be informed whether those seeking donations are volunteers, employees of the organization, or hired solicitors

IX. To have the opportunity for their names to be deleted from mailing lists that an organization may intend to share

X. To feel free to ask questions when making a donation and to receive prompt, truthful, and forthright answers

NOTES

1. © 2015, Association of Fundraising Professionals (AFP), all rights reserved. Reprinted with permission from the Association of Fundraising Professionals.

Appendix D

Training at Your Institution

ATLAS: Academic Training, Leadership, & Assessment Services offers training programs, books, and materials that deal with many aspects of academic leadership, collegiality, and fundraising. Its programs include:

- Decision Making
- Problem Solving
- Work-Life Balance
- Time Management
- Stress Management
- Conflict Management
- Promoting Teamwork
- Promoting Collegiality
- Communicating Effectively
- Leading Meetings Effectively
- Managing Projects Effectively
- Positive Academic Leadership
- Best Practices in Faculty Evaluation
- Creating a Culture of Student Success
- Change Leadership in Higher Education
- The Fundamentals of Academic Leadership
- Going for the Gold: How to Become a World-Class Academic Fundraiser
- World-Class Fundraising Isn't a Spectator Sport: The Team Approach to Academic Fundraising

These programs are offered in half-day, full-day, and multiday formats. ATLAS also offers reduced prices on leadership books and distributes the Collegiality Assessment Matrix (CAM) and Self-Assessment Matrix (S-AM), which allow academic programs to evaluate the collegiality and civility of their faculty members in a consistent, objective, and reliable manner, and other instruments to assess faculty and staff engagement or morale. The monthly ATLAS E-Newsletter addresses a variety of issues related to academic leadership and is sent free to subscribers.

For more information, contact:

ATLAS: Academic Training, Leadership, & Assessment Services
4521 PGA Boulevard, PMB 186
Palm Beach Gardens FL 33418
800-355-6742; www.atlasleadership.com
Email: questions@atlasleadership.com

About the Authors

Jeffrey L. Buller has served in administrative positions ranging from department chair to vice president for academic affairs at four very different institutions: Loras College, Georgia Southern University, Mary Baldwin College, and Florida Atlantic University. He is the author of ten books on higher education administration, a textbook for first-year college students, and a book of essays on the music dramas of Richard Wagner.

Dr. Buller has also written numerous articles on Greek and Latin literature, nineteenth- and twentieth-century opera, and college administration. From 2003 to 2005, he served as the principal English-language lecturer at the International Wagner Festival in Bayreuth, Germany. More recently, he has been active as a consultant to the Ministry of Education in Saudi Arabia, where he is assisting with the creation of a kingdom-wide Academic Leadership Center. Along with Robert E. Cipriano, Dr. Buller is a senior partner in ATLAS: Academic Training, Leadership, & Assessment Services, through which he has presented numerous workshops on academic leadership and fundraising.

Dianne M. Reeves has enjoyed success in three distinct industries and has held leadership positions spanning more than thirty-five years in nursing, small business management/program development, and higher education advancement. She began her development work at the university level as an advisor to legendary football head coach Howard Schnellenberger. Experienced in marketing and development, Ms. Reeves has also worked as a nonprofit consultant and financial systems manager. She has served as a board member for the Palm Beach County Chapter of the Association of Fundraising Professionals and the Planned Giving Council of Palm Beach County and as a member of Executive Women of Palm Beach.

Ms. Reeves believes that each sector of her work experience has molded her philanthropic approach to the whole person by giving her a more complete understanding of psychology, business, and nonprofit priorities. To date, in her development work, she has raised well more than $45 million for Florida Atlantic University. In this capacity, she sees herself as making a major contribution to the mission and vision of that institution. In addition to a master's degree in business administration, Ms. Reeves has earned several professional certifications in fundraising, most notably the Certified Fund Raising Executive (CFRE), Chartered Advisory in Philanthropy (CAP), and Certified Governance Trainer (CGT), and remains involved with numerous professional organizations. Although she has authored numerous articles in nursing, this book and its companion volume are her first publications in the realm of advancement.

CPSIA information can be obtained
at www.ICGtesting.com
Printed in the USA
BVHW041256080719
552863BV00001B/57/P